Sacred Messages

FROM THE GUARDIANS OF THE EARTH

CHANNELED BY DIANE OSVOLD

Reviews

"*Sacred Messages from the Guardians of the Earth* is a visually stunning and profoundly beautiful book. The channeled messages are sincere, thought-provoking, and so needed today. I was most inspired by the messages from Isis, including one that truly hit home for me: 'Do not limit yourself by asking what can I do.' This book is a treasure and its messages and affirmations are a true guide for the world."

—Leslie Sampson, author of Find Your Twin Flame

"*Sacred Messages from the Guardians of Earth*" is equal parts revelation and respite. The themes and messages nourish and comfort the reader as well as inspire hope and understanding. Combined with the visual art, they take the reader on a love and light-filled journey into the mystical realms that are often hard to access. Thank you Diane for sharing this beautiful work of art with the world."

—Dr. Rima Bonario, Teacher, Soul-Coach, and Author of The Seven Queendoms, A SoulMap for Embodying Sacred Feminine Sovereignty

"Diane is a magically gifted intuitive. Her book is full of inspiring messages and artwork that will uplift your spirits and give guidance to your soul. Whenever you feel called, open the book and let it bring you a message from the divine. The message will be exactly what you need."

—Jen Taylor, EEM-CP (Eden Energy Medicine Certified Practitioner)

"I love the Book *Sacred Messages* by Diane Osvold! I love to randomly flip the book open to a different message every day. I feel extremely connected and positive for the day—everytime!"

—Christian Sean Yong, Artist, Owner Intuitive Art Studio

"For the last year, I have been exceptionally blessed to be witness as Diane channeled these great works. Whatever I needed to hear came through. Every single message was always incredibly on point for exactly what was going on at that moment in time. I am so inspired by this book and excited that it's getting into the hands of the world. These messages are inspiring, and the art is uplifting. Diane is a gifted pure channel and has a true connection to the sacred information this world needs to hear. I can hear and feel these messages that she has brought forth in my soul."

—*Michelle Orwick, Spiritual Activator*

"This book is for all who seek to enhance their inner reserves of love, joy, and peace while upgrading their connection to the spiritual realm. There is powerful energy contained within these pages that transcends the words and images. The messages and art contained in Diane's work carry incredibly inspirational confirmations and potent healing. Each communication feels personally directed while remaining universally applicable to all who are fortunate enough to engage with this beautiful tome. What an amazing and magical creation Diane has produced!"

—*Missy Barnes, College Professor, Department Chair, Spiritual Coach and Healer*

"If you are a soul who seeks to be unbound by religious doctrine, yet open to spiritual truth, then this book is for you. The messages are well written and will lift you to new heights. The illustrations, amazingly painted by the author herself, convey their own deep spirituality, and are alone well worth the price of the book. My prayer is that you will be amazed at the level of insight you attain!"

—*Rabbi Dennis Jones, Hickory, North Carolina, USA*

FLOWER of LIFE PRESS

Sacred Messages from the Guardians of the Earth
By Diane Osvold
Copyright © 2023 Diane Osvold

All rights reserved. No part of this publication may be reproduced, distributed, or transmitted in any form or by any means, including photocopying, recording, or other electronic or mechanical methods, without the prior written permission of the publisher. The views and opinions expressed in this publication are those of the author and do not necessarily reflect the views or positions of Flower of Life Press.

Published by Flower of Life Press
Hadlyme, CT
Publisher, Astara J. Ashley
www.FlowerofLifePress.com

For information about special discounts for bulk order purchases, email: support@floweroflifepress.com

Cover and Interior Design: Astara Jane Ashley, www.floweroflifepress.com
Cover and Interior Art: Diane Osvold

Library of Congress Control Number: Available upon request.

ISBN: 979-8-9873954-9-3

This book is dedicated to my late husband John. His passing in the prime of his life cycle sent me on a quest to find the truth behind the eternal soul.

Always in my Heart

Acknowledgments

I would like to thank the Spiritual Beings who entrusted me to deliver their messages. The beautiful paintings would not have come to life without the amazing teaching and artistic talent of my mentor Christian Sean Yong of Intuitive Art Studio. He taught me to believe in my abilities and let go of the idea of perfection in art. He always encouraged me to get the paint on the canvas and see what wonderful things unfolded.

My sons Chas and Curt who at times thought I was a little out there but always encouraged me to follow my heart and do whatever made me happy. I would like to thank Curt for his amazing technical skills. There were so many times he came to my rescue at my computer. It always started out with "Curt I can't…"

Thank you to my mom Betty Atwood for being my biggest cheerleader. She has encouraged me every step along my spiritual path. Every message I shared with her she always claimed it was profound and reiterated that I needed to share these messages with the world. My mom stated "There is more to this life than just the physical world, and Diane's book proves it." Now that's a proud Mom.

To my dad Phil Jones and my Stepmother Mary for always providing me a home away from home in Orlando as I continued to take classes to enhance my spiritual growth.

Thank you to all my friends, fellow soul travelers and mentors that listened as I shared my messages at retreats, workshops and zoom calls. Their encouragement gave me the push I needed to see this book brought to life. Thank you especially to Michell Orwick for always inviting me to share in her Monthly Moon Circle and Mystic Rose program.

A big heartfelt thank you to Astara, my publisher and all the support staff at Flower of Life Press. You made birthing this book a wonderful experience and I look forward to many more.

Contents

Acknowledgments vii
Introduction 1
Meet the Guardians of the Earth 3

Greetings from the Goddess Council ... 11	Mother Earth 57
The Great Goddess 13	Isis 59
Sekhmet 15	Sekhmet 61
Mother Earth 17	Isis 63
Greetings from the Goddess Council ... 11	Fire Goddess 65
The Great Goddess 13	Isis 67
Sekhmet 15	Water Goddess 69
Mother Earth 17	The Goddess Council 71
Mother Mary and Kuan Yin 19	Alleahel Star Being 73
Isis 21	Isis 75
Mother Earth 23	Mary Magdalene 77
Kali 25	Isis 79
Goddess Gaia 27	Melchizedek 81
The Goddess Council 29	The Guardians of the Elements 83
The Great Goddess 31	The Goddess Council 85
Isis 33	Council of 12 87
Morrighan 35	Isis 89
Goddess of Fire 37	The Galactic Council 91
Mother Earth 39	Team in Spirit 93
Isis 41	Element of Air 95
The Galactic Council 43	Master Guide 97
Mary Magdalene 45	The Law of Order and Oneness 99
Isis 47	Council of 12 101
Mother Earth 49	Ascended Masters 103
Isis 51	Ancestors of the Land 105
Pele 53	The Galactic Council 107
Hathor 55	Element of Air 109

Goddess of Fire 113
Sekhmet 115
The Goddess Council 117
The Galactic Council 119
Isis 121
Team in Spirit 123
Spirit Guides 125
Master Guide 127
Radiant Beings of Light 129
The Law of Numbers 131
Dolphin Spirit 133
Spirits of Love 135
Father Tree 137
Spirit of Generosity 139
Ancient Warrior Spirit 141
Master Guide 143
The Watchers 145
The Law of Numbers 147
Isis 149
Spirit of the Wind 151
The Great Goddess 153
Isis 155
Spirit Guide 157
The Realm of Guardian Angels 159

ABOUT THE AUTHOR 161

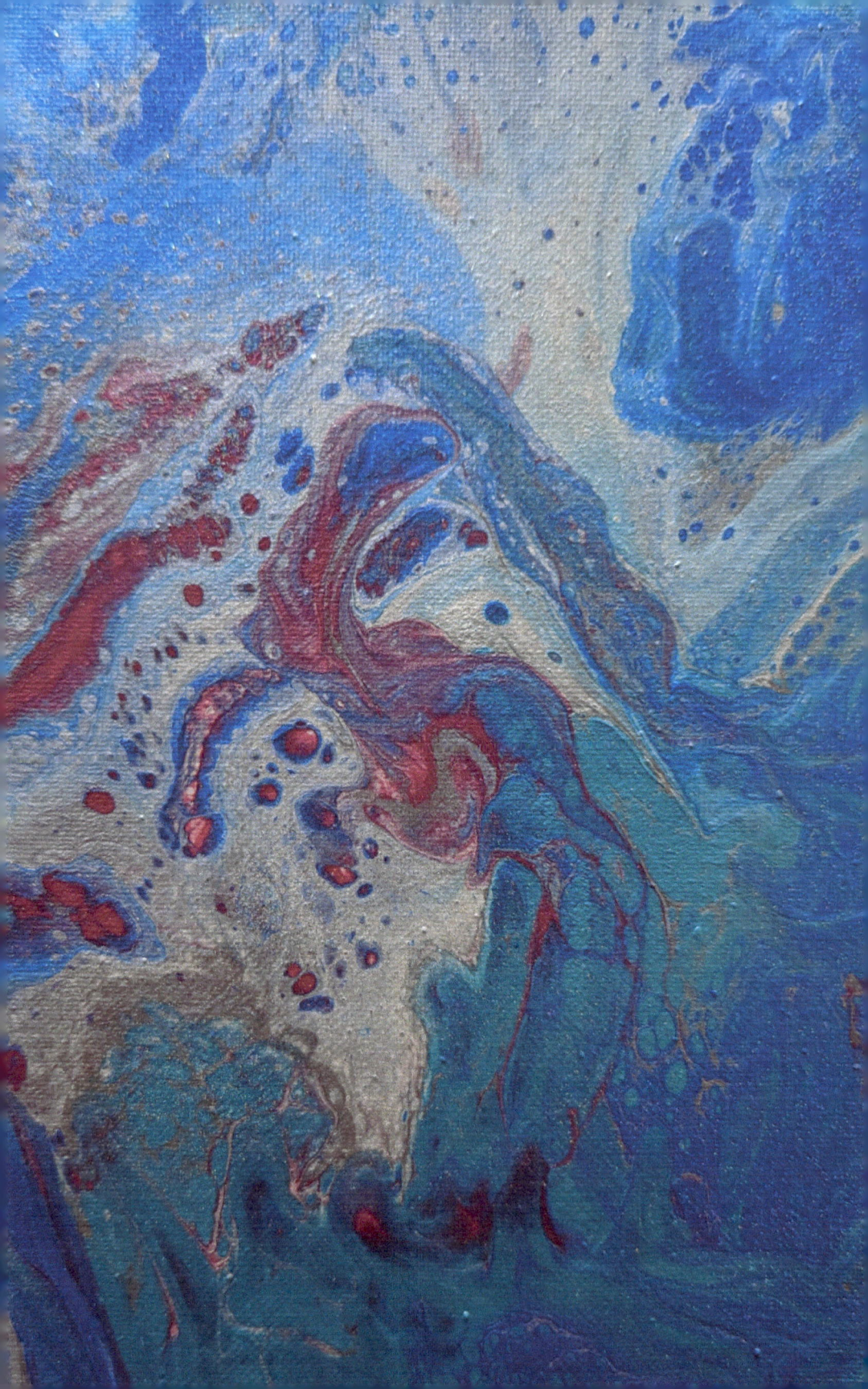

Introduction

One of my favorite sayings that has come through in several messages is

"A spiritual journey is not for the faint of heart."

It would be hard to put a time stamp on when and how long I have been on my spiritual journey. If I truly look back I would say it has been for most of my life, starting as a small child who saw and felt spirits. Then came the intuitive knowing which included knowledge and truths regardless of what someone was saying. This was very helpful raising two sons. I spent most of my twenties and thirties focusing on being a wife and mother, therefore the spiritual journey took a smaller role. When both my children went to school, I returned to college and expanded my learning in different areas. One of my humanities classes really opened my eyes to looking at religion from a historical view. This was just another part of my spiritual journey—understanding other belief systems.

I consider myself a student of life. The lessons were not always easy. It was one such lesson twenty years ago that totally changed my life. The loss of my husband at only thirty-nine was a major turning point. It created a time of not knowing what to believe. I could have easily given up on all things spiritual. Instead, a nighttime visit from him after his passing sent me on a quest to understand what happens to the Soul when a person passes from this earth.

I started on a small scale, reading books and attending local workshops, but the more I learned the more I wanted to know. All of a sudden I found myself on the fast track of my spiritual journey. Soon I was attending workshops, classes and retreats all over the world. I have studied Angels, past lives, several healing modalities, Goddess Mysteries, oracle cards, mediumship and psychic abilities. I learned along the way that I could connect to spirits and bring messages through for others. I have worked with clients as a psychic, medium, healer, and past life regressionist. The more my abilities opened up I began to believe beyond a doubt that the Soul is truly eternal and we are surrounded by our spirit helpers and they want us to live our best lives.

This knowledge and connection became even deeper for me when I started to receive channeled messages. At first, the messages were fairly simple and short, but the more I opened myself up, the longer and deeper the messages became. I would clear and ground my energy and ask if anyone has a message that needed to be shared. I would sit quietly with pen in hand and just start to write as the words come pouring out onto the paper. The messages were always messages of love, hope, peace, and connection.

There have been times along the path of my spiritual journey that I have been asked to be a channel. It was at a retreat in 2020 that Isis first appeared to me and asked me to bring forth her messages. At the time, I was overwhelmed by her energy, but she worked with me to raise my vibration in order to receive her messages. Isis also revealed to me that if I would journey to Egypt, my abilities to receive messages from other Gods and Goddesses would increase—and boy was she right! I was now in receiver mode and the messages came through anytime and anywhere. The messages I received are from a diverse group of Spiritual beings—Goddesses, Ascended Masters, The Galactic Council, Spirit Guides, Ancestors, Guardians, and departed loved ones. Even the private messages I received from my own deceased loved ones are universal and are intended as words of encouragement.

Along with receiving these messages, I have been told that I need to bring these messages to the world. The Council of Twelve confirmed this with a message I received in July of 2022. "We are The Council of Twelve. We are here today to offer you support and guidance. You have been entrusted with a sacred mission. We would not have given you this mission without the means or the help to see it through. We are very pleased with your desire to honor all who have contributed to this collection of sacred messages by wanting to present it to the world in a beautiful way." This book is a collection of these messages. I have also received visions of these sacred beings that I have painted and included with their messages.

My vision for this book is that someone can pick it up and open it to any page to receive the message they need to hear or the vision to meditate upon. This book of sacred messages and art can be used on a daily or weekly basis. Trust that however you choose to use this book is the right way for you. I just know that it is my mission to get these messages out to the people or I would not have been blessed with the ability to receive them.

So dear reader, it is my greatest hope that these words touch your life and fill you with love, hope, peace, and connection.

Meet the Guardians of the Earth

These messages are from such a diverse group of beings I thought it would be helpful to know a little about each one. Instead of just relaying the basic information that can be found to describe them, I decided to go directly to the source. I connected with each being and asked how they wanted to be presented to the world. The following introductions are their channeled responses to my question. What do you want the world to know about you?

Alleahel Star Being

Alleahel is a star being from another galaxy. She appears when a person is open to receive and believes there is life beyond our own planet. She activates a person's inner knowledge. She does this by connecting the pulsating gold star on her forehead to our third eye located in the center of our forehead.

Ancient Native American Fire Goddess

I share the same energy and passion as other Fire Goddesses. I am a giver of life and also I can be the destructor of it. I am referred to as Native American to show the devotion I have to the people who populated these lands for hundreds of years. They worshiped and valued all of life. That is my greatest wish as a Goddess that all will come to this place of reverence. (This Goddess presented herself to me in Mt. Shasta, CA.)

Ancient Warrior Spirit

I represent the spirit of all warriors who have fought to protect their people and their land. We did not do this for sport; this was a very important assignment. We have reverence for all life and only took one when it was the only answer. We always asked the Great Spirit to deliver them safely to their next destination.

Ancestors of the Land

We are the collective spirits of all the people before you that have lived on earth. We are generations that know the importance of living and respecting the land. We know we needed what the earth provided in order to survive. We welcome all who love and respect the land.

Ascended Masters

We are a representation of enlightened beings. This would include spiritual masters such as Jesus, Buddha, Melchizedek, Solomon and many others. Our messages are from a collective group of unity consciousness. We work together in tandem to deliver messages throughout your world. We are here to support and encourage all regardless of their belief system.

Council of Twelve

We are a group of twelve enlightened beings that are assigned to watch over your life path from birth. We gently try to direct you as you make choices in your life, but we cannot interfere with your life. However, we are always available to those who choose to contact and consult with us.

Dolphin Spirit

I am an example of an enlightened being in a form different from your own. We are the keepers of ancient knowledge that we would like to impart on humans. We are a reminder of all that is beautiful and joyful in the waters of the earth. We communicate that joy to all who take time to watch us enjoy our natural environment.

Element of Air/Spirit of the Wind

We represent one of the four physical elements of your earth. We are all important: earth, air, fire, and water. All four are needed to sustain life. We are all a living breathing entity. It is our hope that the people of the earth realize how important the elements are to a well balanced life.

Father Tree

I am a living, breathing being. I have physical feelings and emotional feelings. I feel the sun, wind, and rain on my leaves and branches. I feel my connectedness to all the other trees, plants, and animals. I feel the emotions of the humans around me. I carry the wisdom from many lifetimes in my cell memory. My Spirit is eternal just like yours.

Guardian Angels

We have been depicted through time as beings with wings. We are a diverse group of beings designed by the Creator. There are Angels of all shapes and sizes with different functions. As Guardian Angels, we are assigned to watch over an individual and assist them when they ask for our help and protection.

Guardians of the Elements

We are spirit beings that oversee and protect the elements of earth, fire, water, and air. We work to keep the elements pure and in balance. We encourage the people of the earth to work with us to keep this beautiful planet clean. Imbalances in the elements create what you call natural disasters, as earth seeks to regain its balance.

Goddess of Fire

There have been many Fire Goddesses in many different cultures. We have been called different names in each one. We are a Goddess essence that is part of the original creation that started with a burst of energy. We bring our gift of fire to ignite a burning passion for life.

Hathor

I am an Egyptian Goddess of healing. I am often seen on temple walls performing ceremonies with Isis. We worked together to bring healing to all people. Like other Goddesses, my name and face has changed over the centuries, but I am still available to call upon for healing in your life.

Isis/The Great Goddess

I am Isis. I am best known as an Egyptian Goddess of life and resurrection. I am a Goddess essence that has been in existence since the beginning of time. My name and face have changed many times throughout the existence of humankind, but my primary goal is to teach love, acceptance, and generosity toward all humans and this beautiful planet.

Kali

I am a Hindu Goddess of fire. I am often portrayed as a Goddess of destruction, but this is not an accurate portrayal. I am the Goddess who gifted the humans with fire for warmth and cooking. My energies are boundless and the destruction is so that something greater can be created.

Kuan Yin

I am a Goddess not limited by boundaries. I have been worshiped in China for many centuries. I am a giver of life—the loving, nurturing caregiver of the ultimate mother energy. I am here to relieve the suffering of all mankind.

Mary Magdalene

I am the embodiment of a loving and nurturing mother. I have unconditional love that is not limited by time and space. I have been misrepresented in the past. My mission in my lifetime was to teach love of God, each other, and our beautiful planet. My mission in spirit form is to continue these teachings to all who call upon me for help. I am not limited by the constraints of your world. I can help you achieve a life full of love.

Master Guide

Each person is assigned a group of guides on the other side to watch over and assist them in their lifetime. As a Master Guide, I am the one in charge of all the Spirit Guides. I oversee all the activities as a person lives their life and searches for their soul purpose in this incarnation. For contact with me and the other guides, is up to the individual to call upon us.

Melchizedek

I am an ancient priest. I walked this earth many centuries ago. I am a keeper of knowledge and wisdom. I work with sacred geometry to teach about patterns and balance. These ancient symbols are the key to manifesting and abundance. I am available to all who call upon me for my guidance and wisdom. It does not matter what your belief system is. The Ascended Masters are a resource for all.

Morrighan

I am an ancient Celtic Goddess. I have existed since the beginning of creation. I am the Goddess of death and rebirth. I welcome my children back into my womb to be reborn in another lifetime. I am the mother of all creation.

Mother Earth/Gaia

I am the living breathing aspect of the planet. I am the nurturer and protector of all life forms upon your earth. I embody the systems of living in harmony with all. My essence is what keeps everything in balance and regeneration.

Mother Mary

I am the mother of Jesus, an Ascended Master who walked the face of this earth spreading his message of love. I continue to share his message of love to all people of the earth. I am a loving, nurturing, and caring representative of mothering energy.

Pele

I am known as a Hawaiian Fire Goddess. I was created from the ashes of volcanic fire. I am the keeper of volcanoes and the islands that they form. I am a giver of life upon these lush islands. I will protect my islands at all costs.

Radiant Beings of Light

We are often seen as angels. We are beings that were created by the Divine to support the higher energies of the enlightened ones. We were created with a vibrational frequency that can keep the energy of your planet in balance.

Sekhmet

I am an Egyptian Goddess often depicted with the head of a lion. I am a healer and keeper of ancient knowledge. I have been in existence from before written records. I was once worshiped for my wisdom. Priestesses used my healing arts on the people of Egypt.

Spirit Guides

We are a group of divine beings who agree, before a human incarnates on the planet, to watch over and guide them along their life path. Many of us have existed on Earth and on many other planets. We know what it is like to transverse both worlds. (The messages in this book are from the author's personal Spirit Guides.)

Spirit of Generosity

We do not like to be defined by words, but by action. We are the living example of acts of kindness, generosity, love, and giving. These beautiful deeds create a high vibration frequency that raises your vibration and creates a cycle of positivity and generosity in action.

Spirit of the Land

Everything has a soul. We represent all the solid formations of your planet that vibrate at a lower frequency. We are the keepers of the rocks, sand, ground, mountains, canyons, and dirt. We have the energy imprint of everything that has occurred upon the land masses. We chose to reveal ourselves to this Oracle (the author) in Hawaii.

Team in Spirit

We are a group of Spiritual beings on the other side of the veil. We include Spirit Guides, Angels, Deceased Loved Ones, and Ancestors. We are honored to work with individuals on their life path, and help them with our combined knowledge and skills that we have gained through our experiences. This collective group is the personal team of the author. However, everyone has their own team they can call upon.

The Galactic Council

We are a group of collective beings from other planets and star systems. We are gathered together to watch over planetary safety. We use our collective energies to keep your planet from destructive powers.

The Goddess Council

We are a collective group of Goddess essences and ideals. We are here to impart our knowledge to the collective to bring them into a place of peace in their lifetime. We are a representation of all the good that is in each and every Goddess that has taught and cared for their people.

The Law of Love and Oneness

We are one of the Universal Laws. We represent the connectedness of all peoples and all things. You are all connected to the vibration of love. The frequency of the love vibration can be used for healing, balance, and harmony.

The Law of Numbers

We are one of the Universal Laws. We represent an endless combination of numbers. Our essence is a creation of structure and order. All matter is a vibrational frequency and these frequencies are made up of numbers.

The Spirits of Love

We represent the frequency of love. It is the collective energy of all types of love be it romantic, parental, spiritual, or love of nature. When humans express love, the energy raises the frequency of love across all time and space. We gather this energy and focus it on areas of unrest. The Spirit of Love is a healing balm applied where it is needed most.

The Watchers

We are an army of celestial beings. We are assigned to watch over and protect a planet that has life forms on it. We are only allowed to send our beam of heart-centered light for protection. The purpose of this loving beam is to connect all with unconditional love.

Water Goddess

I am a representation of all life-giving waters. I am the spirit found in oceans, ponds, rivers, lakes, and streams. I am always moving and changing. I provide life-giving water to all creatures upon your earth.

Greetings from the Goddess Council

We bring you a message of hope.

Focus on the positive things in your life. There is too much focus on low-vibration messages and material items. Love, light, and high vibrations are what is going to save the earth. Be a being of hope and love spreading the peace and joy everywhere you go and to everyone you meet. The supply of love is unlimited! Share it!

The Goddess of the East and Air wishes you to spread your wings and fly. Know that anything is possible if you just believe in yourself. Do not listen to those who would keep you grounded. I am telling you to reach for the stars. Your source of love and creation is unlimited. You are the one who puts limitations on yourself.

The Goddess wants you to be that shining example of a life lived to its fullest. Show the world the unending power of the Goddess—the Goddess within and the Goddess without. Never stop believing you were put here to help bring in the Divine Feminine to help balance the Divine Masculine. They are equal in all forms and should be taught that way to the younger generations. Now is the age of balance!

AFFIRMATION

I am an unlimited source of love and creation.

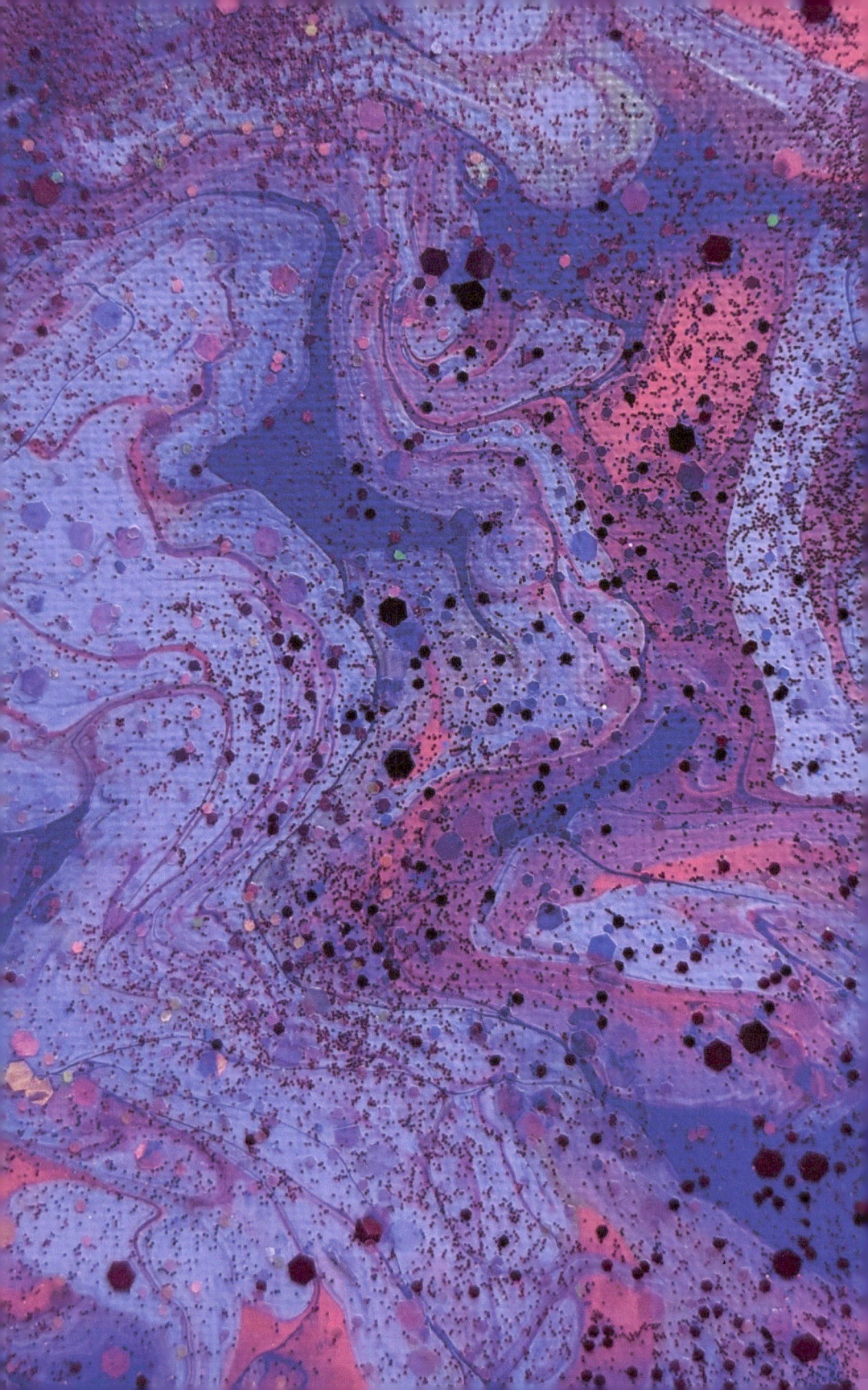

The Great Goddess

Children of the earth, release your sorrow.

All is not lost. There are beings all around you working for the good of mankind. There are people of the earth who work behind the curtain to bring about a lasting peace.

It may feel very dark and heavy right now, but that is always the case before a breakthrough. Even the medical crisis is not enough to overturn all the good that is being done. The souls involved with this agreed to be here for it. It would be so much easier if you only remembered what you agreed to: to elevate your soul. However, this knowledge would create another level of confusion for those stuck in the third dimension. That is why as you work to elevate your soul during your life you are given access to the Akashic records, spirit guides, and Ascended Masters. You have leveled up enough to use and understand this information without going crazy.

Continue to embrace the spirit connections and the psychic abilities. It is through this growing and evolving process you are using your newfound knowledge for your good and the good of all. Keep being an open vessel to Spirit and everyone will share in the rewards.

AFFIRMATION

I am connected to the Spirit realm.

Sekhmet

Your world is a wonderful place.

There is so much there that you can enjoy. Nature brings healing to all creatures and all you have to do is sit and be still. Enjoy the sights and the sound and they do the healing for you. All that is asked in return is that you treat every living thing with respect and be grateful for the bounty of nature. The forest, oceans, mountains and meadows have been created for your benefit.

It saddens us to think that so many are focused on the material possessions of your world. The greatest gift is before your eyes and it is free. No one really owns the earth. You are just given the privilege of being on the earth for a very short time. Acceptance of this knowledge is what will bring lasting peace and joy. There is always a spot in nature that a person can go to for free and drink in all the beautiful healing and peace it has to offer. So simple of a concept but so hard for the masses to grasp. All they have to do is look around them to see the true beauty and freedom in our words.

Do not tie yourself to the material world. You will never find that which you seek. Embrace the beauty of the natural world and you will feel the bond of your 3D world dissolve. There is beauty all around you but the greatest beauty lives within you.

AFFIRMATION

I drink in the beauty of Mother Earth that surrounds me and I am one with it.

Mother Earth

This is the dawning of a new age.

It is a new way of looking at things. It is a new way that is looking to the old ways of living in harmony with Mother Earth and each other.

The time has come to create a world that we were brought here to create. Release the fear, anger and resentments. Embrace the joy, peace and love. Others will follow this example.

It is okay to create this in your own life and your own space. Do not worry about what other people think. Do not fall into the low vibration of judgment.

There is a perfect world waiting to be created. Start it today in your own little corner of the world. Fill it with beautiful things that bring you peace and joy. It will help you to be more creative. Remember, dear ones, you are the co-creators of this world. The power of numbers is on your side. There have never been so many lightworkers on the planet at one time and there have never been so many ways to reach out to one another. Join hands and hearts with your brothers and sisters and truly bring in the Age of Aquarius.

AFFIRMATION

I live in harmony with all.

Mother Mary and Kuan Yin

This is a message of compassion and love from Mother Mary and Kuan Yin.

They are here today as a unified force to show how we all need to come together. It does not matter where we are on our spiritual journey or if the person is just living their life in the third dimension. We need to show them love and compassion right where they are.

Do not look to others for the evolution of your Soul. It is your choice and responsibility. If someone does not choose this evolution for themselves, bless them and move on. We are responsible for each other through soul connection and love, but we cannot make choices or decisions for them. The best you can do is show them that living an elevated life through your connection with Spirit is the road to happiness. Each and everyone of us has to do the work and with the work comes the reward.

Respect each other for their choices and release all judgment. It does not serve you or them; it only lowers the vibration of the whole planet. Choose love and compassion for all and show the world this is the path to peace on earth.

Lovingly, your Mothers

AFFIRMATION

I choose to share love and compassion with everyone.

Isis

Goddesses of the Earth, heed my call.

This is the time of the great awakening and the call to return to the way of the Goddess. The way of the Goddess is honoring your femininity and living in harmony with the earth. It is not about where someone is on their spiritual path and who is further along. It is about coming together as sisters to help and support each other. There are too few of you really living in alignment with each other. We are all connected. When one is hurting, hungry, or suffering in sorrow, we all are.

This is your call to rise up and become one. The littlest thing you do to help someone will return to you tenfold. This is a beautiful cycle that allows you to reach out to all your sisters. Do not limit yourself by asking what can I do. If you see a need, fill it. If you see suffering, ease the pain. If you see hunger, feed the hungry. These little acts gain momentum. Soon you will be living in a world of love, appreciation, and wonder. It is not beyond your abilities. This is a time to think small and let it build from there. We are here to balance the energies of lack and proclaim this new age, new way, and new world. Abundance for all!

AFFIRMATION

My abundance touches everyone in my life.

Mother Earth

This is a message of hope!

Our hope is that humanity will wake up and honor all they have been given. Not only are they Divine beings with miraculous abilities, they have been given stewardship of this beautiful planet. This does not mean that they are given free range to abuse and destroy the wonders of nature. It means that they are to love and care for the planet and all living forms on it—from the plants, animals, and human beings, to the rivers, rocks, mountains, and oceans!

It is a symbiotic relationship. It needs to be a relationship of mutual respect and honor. We have taken so much, now is the time to give back. One person can perform miracles. Take care of your small piece of earth and it will give back to you. Clean up your environment, reuse, and recycle. Conserve the natural resources and respect the life-giving elements of earth, air, water, and fire. They are not unlimited, but they are resilient. Without human interference, they will clean and purify themselves. They existed before us, and they will be here long after we are gone. Love and respect what has been trusted to your care, and know that it will be returned to you. Mother Earth will cradle you in her womb.

AFFIRMATION

*I conserve natural resources
in order to sustain life on earth.*

Kali

The Goddess of the Earth is here today to say thank you for the care and respect that you give to Mother Earth.

Every time you recycle, pick up trash, and repurpose things, you are honoring our Earth Mother.

Our Earth Mother is a powerful force, but she needs our help to keep her running smoothly. Too many man-made products are polluting her waters and her lands. Be mindful of what you have been given. As all Souls on the earth are connected to each other we are also connected to the Earth Mother. Everyone talks about the silver cord that connects your soul to your body, but no one talks about the green cord that connects you to Mother Earth. This is a lifeline that keeps the good energy from the heart of the earth running through your body.

This is a call to take care of your body also. Provide it with good food and water. Walk it and release physical and emotional toxins. There is a direct connection to those who honor their bodies and their deep respect for this earth. Wake up the world to this connection. We can only move forward together. The love and care we give to each other and the earth will be returned tenfold. Start in your small corner of the world and watch it become a global movement.

AFFIRMATION

The respect I show the earth is reflected back to me.

Goddess Gaia

We are coming to you once again as emissaries of the land.

It is our job to reach out to all who will heed this call. Now is the time for the people of the earth to take pride in their stewardship of this beautiful planet. There are many souls who would love to be on a planet such as this. Take care of what you have been gifted and save it for future souls that will be incarnating on this planet. Everything you need is right here. It has everything you need to sustain life: air, water, fire, and earth. From the things that grow on the earth to the things that swim in the ocean, you have an abundance of what you need as long as you respect it as the life-giving element that it is.

It also has everything you need to heal your bodies. You do not need to turn to false chemicals. Mother Nature will provide what your body needs to heal itself. There are many on your earth right now that are bringing in the information of plant medicine. Listen to them with an open heart and discern what resonates with you. Be in charge of your body, just like your planet and it will take care of you. There is no end to the wonders that this wonderful planet has to offer. Offer it your love and care, and it will offer you a long life.

AFFIRMATION

I take pride in my stewardship of this beautiful planet.

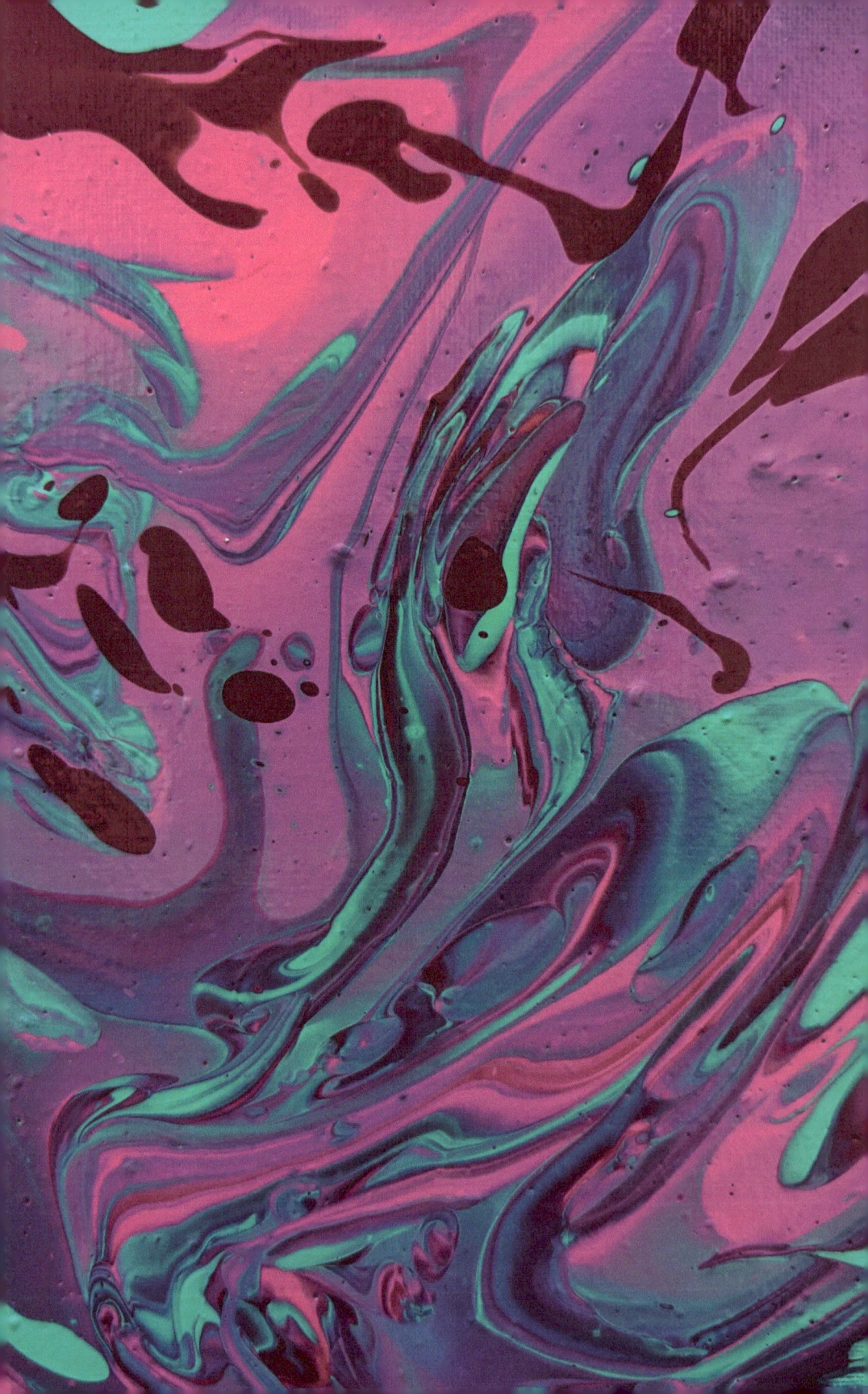

The Goddess Council

The Goddesses want you to know that you are not serving anyone by taking on others' troubles and drama.

You have learned enough of your own lessons. It is not your purpose to take on another's lessons or carry their burdens for them. When you do this, you rob them of the gift of learning for themselves and overcoming obstacles. You also rob yourself of the peace and joy you have earned for yourself. It is not out of lack of love that you release others' burdens, but a place of self-love to ease your own.

When you open yourself up to true peace and joy, you will bring more balance to the world around you. Do not let others dim your light. Let them be warmed by it. The greatest gift we can give ourselves and others is unconditional love and understanding. Be the anchor of love and light, not the anchor of other burdens. The Goddess provides love and support but we must find our own answers and our own way.

AFFIRMATION

I am an anchor for love and light.

The Great Goddess

Take heart dear child, your prayers have been heard and are being answered.

Yours is a special purpose that cannot be put on hold any longer. The information you are receiving needs to be shared with the world. There are so many in need and in doubt. They need to hear and read the loving words of the Masters. Words of hope, words of encouragement and words of love are what is going to propel this world forward and into its highest accession. It can no longer be powered by greed and corruption. The days of being out of balance are coming to an end. We are entering the age of peace and harmony. Those who cannot live by these principles will choose to leave this plane. The people who come together in love and support for each other will create a world of high vibration and miracles.

Be patient, my dear loved ones. A change of this magnitude will still take more time. Create more love and peace in your own space and with your loved ones. This will sustain you until we can reach a state of world peace. Do not listen to false messages or low-vibration people. It is all part of the illusion to keep you from claiming your birthright. A right of a life filled with love, light, joy, and peace. Just remember that these things must start with you in order to be passed on to another. Love in all things.

AFFIRMATION

I vibrate in the frequency of peace and love.

Isis

Goddesses of the Earth, heed my call.

Arise, my Beloved and claim your birthright. You did not come here to suffer and experience lack. You came here to be a beautiful being of light and love. Those of you who are remembering this are now claiming your birthright. No longer will you let anyone or anything dim your light. You have the ability to manifest anything your heart desires. That is the secret. It has to come from the heart and a desire to make this world a better place.

Selfish desires may be fulfilled, but they will never be filling. Your Soul knows what it truly needs to live a fulfilled life. When you fill your life up with unconscionable things you are just delaying your true Divine purpose. Simplify your life! Get rid of what no longer serves your highest and best and you will make room for miracles to happen.

Do not put a material value on manifesting, it goes so much deeper than what you see. When you manifest a life of soul purpose you raise the vibrations of the whole planet and everyone on it. It is through these vibrations and the frequency of love that we will not only survive this accession process, we will thrive. Claim your birthright my dear ones and start living, spreading and embodying a soul filled magnificent life.

Lovingly, Isis, The Mother of All Time!

AFFIRMATION

I manifest the life of my Soul purpose.

Morrighan

I am the Goddess Morrighan.

I also have been called by many names. Most believe I am the Goddess of death and battle. This is sadly mistaken. I am the loving mother who watches her children grow into adults and forget that we are all connected. The children become men and women who thirst for power and I must be here to clean up the mess. That is why I am often spotted in war-torn areas. Just like the Raven who waits for the carnage to be over. I wait for mankind to come to their senses and start treating each other better. More is gained through love and peace then hate and battle. There is an awakening at this time by many who now realize this is not the way to preserve life on this planet.

I have been waiting for enough of these Souls to come forward before I was ready to reveal myself. We must break through all the old stereotypes. Especially those surrounding the Goddesses. The Goddesses are a representation of a loving, nurturing mother that only turns fierce when their loved ones are threatened. Too many times our natures have been reshaped by men to push their own agendas. We need to return to the true meaning of the Goddesses in order to bring about balance and harmony. Each Goddess is stepping forward at this time to reveal their true nature and purpose. Please be open to receiving this information and correcting the wrong that has been done to so many of us. You are the generation to make this happen. You are awakening to the Goddess in each one of you and this awakening brings forth the true meaning of the Goddess.

AFFIRMATION

I bring forth the Goddesses as loving, nurturing mother energy.

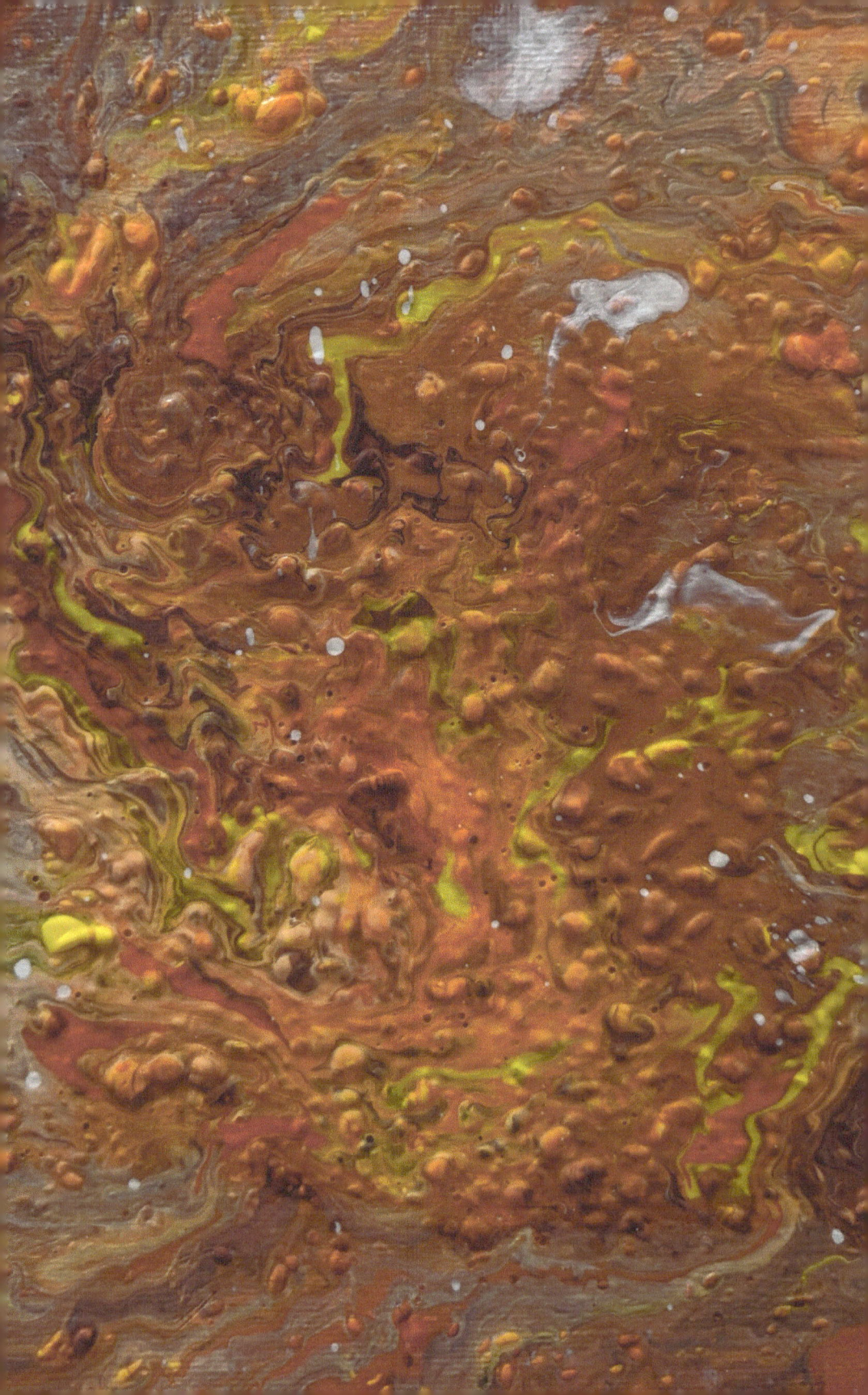

Goddess of Fire

Goddess of the South and fire, I am here with you today to encourage you to find your passion and excitement.

Burn brightly so all will want to know where your secret fire comes from. Not a fire to consume but a fire to illuminate the darkness and show others the way to a life filled with energy and passion. Do not let anyone or anything dim your fire.

You are a unique being of light. A way-shower for all those lost in darkness. Do not fear the unknown for your fire and your light will dispel any low vibrations you come up against. There is no darkness your light cannot penetrate. Your fire and passion is a creative force. Use it to create the life you are meant to live and the love you are meant to give.

AFFIRMATION

I burn with the passion of creativity.

Mother Earth

May the people of the earth realize that all things are sacred.

The plants, animals, trees, rivers, lakes, oceans, mountains, rocks, and even the grains of sand upon the beach. Nothing is put here by accident. They are all living things in their own right. They are put on this earth for their specific purpose. Do not limit yourself to just what you can see, hear, feel and taste. There is a world beyond your five senses that is much larger than your world of perception. Open yourself up to the unknown and the unseen, then you are truly experiencing life.

Have reverence for all things. Be thankful and gracious for what they contribute to your life. You were taught to be thankful for your food, but what of the trees that were used to build your home? Have you ever thanked them for their sacrifice? To be truly grateful and thankful is to go deep, beyond what you have been taught, and thank everything that makes your life better. The seen and the unseen. When you truly appreciate all that Creator/Creatrix has placed upon this magnificent planet, you step into the role of nurturer. As the nurturer, you want only the highest and best for your charges. Only you can decide how you will treat all things upon this earth, thus determining how long you will live in peace and harmony.

AFFIRMATION

I am open to the unknown beyond my five senses.

Isis

My dear sweet child, release your sorrows and burdens upon my shoulders.

I have the strength of ten thousand Goddesses to support and love you. Though this day may seem dark and heavy, there are brighter days ahead. Keep the faith, keep believing that there is a larger picture out there, and you are each a part of it. When you have done your part, you are gathered back to the mother of all, there to decide your next part in bringing the Golden Age to fruition.

Rejoice when it is your time and embrace your next great adventure. There is no need to fear. That which awaits you on the other side is more glorious than words can describe. The freedom of not being confined by a human body is beyond your comprehension. Think of a time in your life where you felt sheer bliss and joy. That is only a small molecule of how you will feel when released from the burdens of this life.

My dear ones, do not let your sorrow and sadness take you out of alignment with your higher vibration. The Spirits on the other side gather together to welcome all who crossover. It is a celebration of a life well lived and the lessons that were mastered. Keep your heart light and remember the veil is thin and that we are all still with you. Love will outlast all!

AFFIRMATION

I am always connected to my loved ones on the other side of the veil.

The Galactic Council

We have created a spiral of protection around the earth.

There is no need for fear and panic. These emotions will only aid the darkness by lowering yours and the collective vibration. Call upon the forces of light and love to remain in a vibration of peace and calm. The benefit to you and all humankind is immeasurable. Wake up and realize the power you have for change. Change how you are thinking and this will change your and your environment's energy. This change for the good will then be reflected in those around you. This truly is a ripple effect for birthing a new way of being. We know you don't see it from our viewpoint. Yours is a small perception, but the change is great.

Each lightworker anchoring the energy where they are is spreading like a warm glow across the whole earth. Envision in your mind a soft golden glow encircling your planet—that is what we see from our perspective. Claim that golden glow and the energy that it emits for your own. See yourself and your home encased with it. The power of the collective love is stronger than any lower-vibration emotion. Bask in this love and the glory that is becoming the Golden Age of peace and enlightenment for all who will rise up and claim it. It is available for all. You just have to release any low vibrations that would weigh you down.

This is the time of your magnificence. This is the time for you to shine and let all peoples of the earth know you are operating in the place of love for all and nothing can hold you back or stop you from spreading the love and light to all who seek. Go in love, go in your magnificence, and raise the vibration with us.

AFFIRMATION

The energies of love and light keep me in alignment with peace and calm.

Mary Magdalene

Now is the time dear ones, to bring to fruition all that you have been working towards and claiming.

Start that healing career, teach that class, and write those books. There is such a need on your planet for this information. Many are waking from their slumber and they will need teachers and mentors to help them along their Spiritual path. You know as well as anyone how difficult this path can be. It is not for the faint of heart. Remember how many lightworkers have crossed your path to get you to this point. Now is the time for you to return the favor.

You have chosen this time on earth because your Soul wants to bring the message of Divine love to all. Your Divine Mission statement is to spread love and light. The best way to do this is to share your knowledge with the world. The more you share, the more you raise the vibration for everyone.

Do not question yourself, and do not question whether you are doing enough. Just by being yourself, you are doing enough. All the other extras that you bring with you are for the enlightenment of man/womankind. Do not ever question your purpose. For you have already fulfilled that by being here now. Go spread your love and light and share with all who are open to receive.

AFFIRMATION

My Divine Mission is to spread love and light.

Isis

I am the Goddess of 10,0000 names.

    I have walked this earth too many times to number. I am here today to bring you a message of peace and love, even though the world seems dark and full of anger, fear, and worry. There are more people than you could count who are anchoring in the light. A universal message of love, light, peace, and harmony is being transmitted to every corner of your Earth.

Even though I am not walking the earth at this time in human form, I am orchestrating more from my dimension. I am calling all daughters of Isis to remember who they are. As we speak I am sending light codes to those who are still asleep. Imagine a brilliant web of light strands encircling your earth. Each time another soul is activated, the lights shine brighter. Those who are aware and know their light codes are activated are bringing more sisters into the fold.

Those flashes of light you see around you are not a problem with your human eyes. It is another soul awakening to this activation. We have been here since the beginning of time and we will be here long after this earth has expired. But take heart, this will not happen for millions of years. Long after the Golden Age and the accession of the earth and the earth souls.

Keep spreading the light and sharing this amazing journey with all who have ears to listen and eyes to see. Each soul that follows this path is like a shining diamond in a crown. It is a crown that can be worn by all. Each and every soul is as special and important as the next. Do not forget this and embrace and treat everyone as the Goddess that they are!

You are embraced and surrounded by my love and my gift of life. I am the Eternal Goddess Isis. I am empowering you—you are becoming impervious to any and all that stand in your way.

AFFIRMATION

I am a sparkling beam of love and light.

Mother Earth

I am the Great Mother.

Lay all your cares and burdens upon me. I will always be here for you. It is a shame that more people do not realize that I have the power to remove what no longer serves you. Even more amazing, I have the power to fill you back up with love, light, and healing.

You are meant to live a life of wholeness, which includes love, health, and prosperity. Too many people are hung up on material wealth, but there is so much more. The smile from a loved one, the laughter of a baby, and a full belly after a good meal. The more you are thankful for the simple things, the more you learn to appreciate all that this life has given you.

Celebrate the simple pleasures, love without constraints, and value the precious time you have been given on this earth. Embrace the beauty all around you. Use all your senses to see, hear, feel, taste, and smell what life is offering you at this banquet. Once you open up to all that has been given to you, you will no longer face this life from a place of lack. I am here to tell you there is plenty to go around. So share with your fellow man from this feast. You are truly provided for.

AFFIRMATION

I celebrate the simple pleasures in my life.

Isis

You are never alone.

I know sometimes it feels like you are the only one on this journey. Take heart, dear one, for many have walked this path before you and pondered the same thing. I am here to tell you that we are here watching your every step and lifting you up along the way. Just remember there have been many times we have pointed you in the right direction. It could be something as simple as a book to read or as complex as orchestrating someone to come into your life. Think back to a time when your life suddenly seemed to change for the better. I am sure looking back you will see that you were Divinely guided in your choices.

Trust as you walk this Spiritual path that you will find the right people to enhance your life. Do not shy away from putting yourself out there. Share your light and your gifts with the world. It is when you share from a place of love and freedom that you truly learn why you are on this journey. We are all connected to those in human form and those in Spirit, and that is why you are never alone.

We are one, we are love, we are eternal!

AFFIRMATION

The changes in my life are Divinely guided.

Pele

I am the primordial Goddess Pele.

I was formed in the fires of a volcano. I am the protector of my beloved islands. Once there were many more then you see now, but my beloved people did not always make the right choices. But there are many here right now that are trying to return to reclaim what was lost.

I am here today speaking to you in hopes of sharing this message. If you are called to this land, then know you were once among the peoples of Lemuria. Your calling goes beyond the desire to sit on beautiful beaches or swim among the waves. Your desire is to bring healing to the land and appease the ancestors who came before you.

I am here today to welcome you to the land flowing with water and lava. You are here to anchor in the energy of the highest vibrations. You are truly Priestesses of a forgotten time. As you stand upon the land, the memories will come flooding back to you. You will remember an ancient way of healing and being. Each one of you is bringing your special magic back with you. All you have to do is claim it. I wait in excited anticipation of your return. May we teach each other the true meaning of being the Priestess in Paradise. Do not fear our reunion. I burn with a fierce passion that I wish to share with you. You will not be consumed in fire but purified by it.

AFFIRMATION

I am a Priestess anchoring the energy of healing into the land.

Hathor

This is a message to the peoples of the earth.

We may no longer walk among you, but our presence and magic are still strong. We are here to support you in times of need, but also to cheer you on in times of celebration. The healing work from the Spiritual plane is always in motion. Combined with the number of Lightworkers on your planet, it creates an impregnable force.

Do not lose faith and do not lose hope. The power in the numbers is what will save humanity. Be a force for good. Spread the love and compassion among your fellow humans. Love and respect your planet for sustaining your life. Be open and fearless on your Spiritual path. There are many Gods and Goddesses; each one represents a force for good. You do not have to limit yourself to just one or one belief. The more you embrace the Gods and Goddesses, the more you become enlightened. The enlightened beings are the ones who see from a place of love, compassion, and tolerance. There is no room for judgment, there is no room for hate. There is only room for love and understanding.

Keep moving on your path of enlightenment and the Gods and Goddesses will help clear the way.

In love always, Hathor

AFFIRMATION

I embrace love, compassion and understanding from all Spiritual Beings.

Mother Earth

Seashells could teach us so much about each other.

They have a hard shell on the outside. They come in all different shapes and colors. Some are fancy and some are plain, but inside is a soft living creature. They thrive in the living waters of the world, and when their time is over, they create beautiful sand beaches. Some shells are found whole and intact and we carry them home to beautify our space.

Each Soul on this planet is here just like the seashell. Some will leave behind a lifetime of service to others. Some Souls will be remembered for the beauty they added to our world. Others will come back again to be sure the message of all is one is not forgotten.

So remember, if you have a hard exterior or are colorful and different, you have a place here on Mother Earth. You add to the uniqueness of our ever-growing and ever-changing world. You are someone special and you have brought joy to someone's life. Sparkle and grow!

AFFIRMATION

Each unique Soul adds their beauty to our world.

Isis

Daughters of the Nile, you are like the lotus flower.

You have been buried beneath the mud of this life, and yet it could not keep you down. You have risen through the layers to become the beautiful bloom I see today. The beauty that I see goes deep within you. Relish yourself and embrace the beauty within. Do not limit yourself by the outside world's definition of beauty. Your beautiful Soul is beyond definition.

Take your amazing gifts and use them on yourself first. This is not selfish; this is self-love. Then it is up to you whether you choose to share your gifts with others. We are here to help and support others, but it is a choice. Choose wisely and do not deplete yourself. Choose from a place of love, choose from a place of pleasure and choose from a place of knowing. Embrace the beauty of choosing. I am with you always.

AFFIRMATION

I choose to rise above all adversity like the beautiful lotus flower.

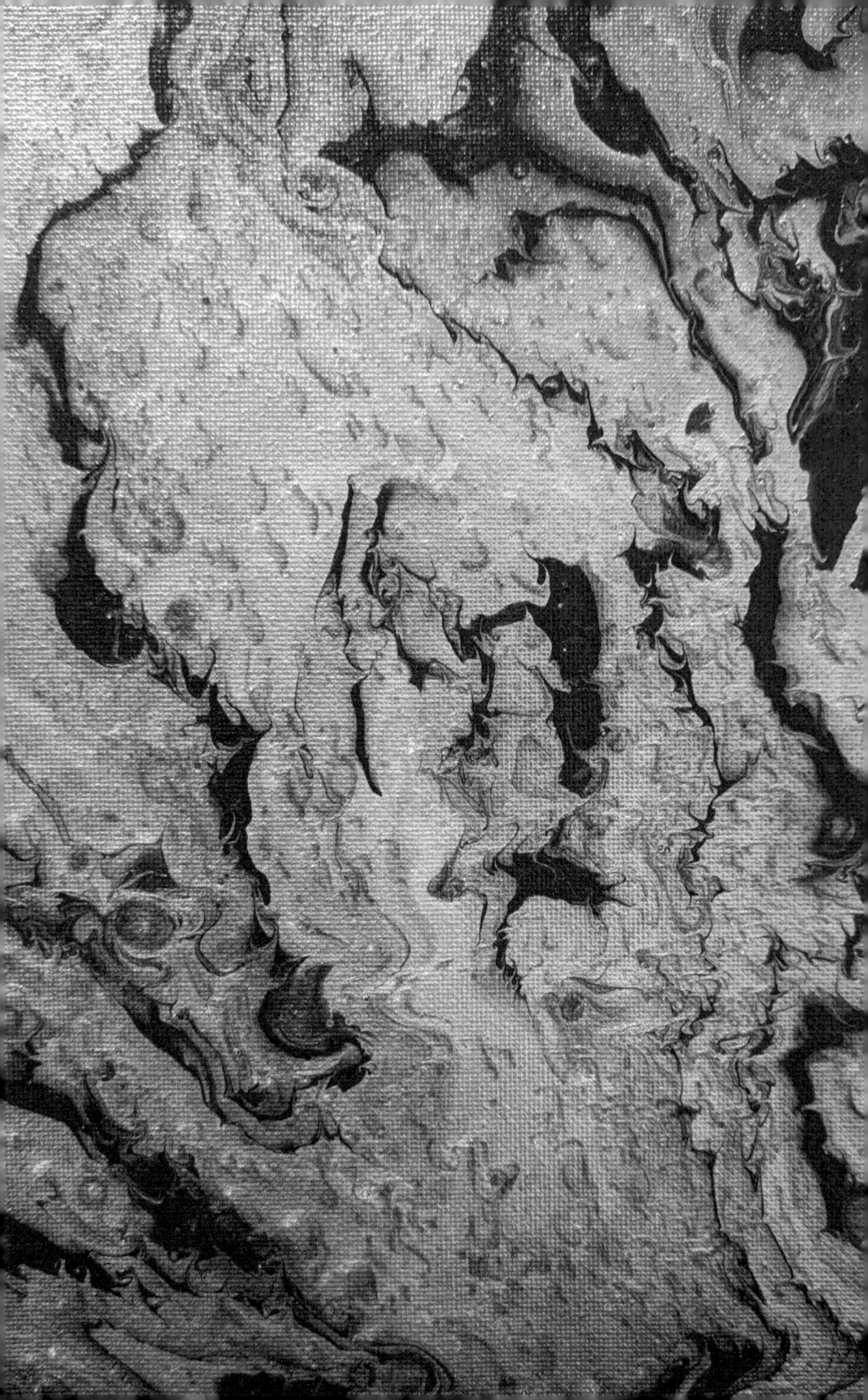

Sekhmet

You are right, Dear Ones—there is a lot of chaotic energy on your earth right now.

It is a time of prophecy where people stuck in the third dimension cannot handle the energy of Mother Earth's ascension. There are those doing violent acts against one another, those choosing to leave this plane, and those choosing to stay and grow with the birthing of this new earth and its ascension vibration.

You are among those choosing to stay. Though it may seem rocky right now, it will soon level out and come to a place of peace. Just remember during this time to take care of yourself first. Practice extreme self-care and keep your vibration high. This will help you to be that beacon for those searching to join the new earth. Let the low-vibration people and things fall away from your life. This is the natural order of things. Do not feel guilty. Remember it is by choice, yours to remain high vibration and others choosing not to do the work.

Take this time to be creative. There is no limit to your ability to create, whether it is a work of art, music, food, or a balanced life. It is all a creation. Remember you are not alone in this endeavor. Your creative partner is Creator, your team in Spirit, and all the ancestors who came before you. They are cheering you on to create the life you desire. The peaceful world you wish to live in and abundance for all. Love is the generator to manifesting all this and more.

Love and light to you, Sekhmet

AFFIRMATION

I choose to be here now, ascending and creating with the new world.

Isis

My dear ones, this is a message of healing for the peoples of the earth.

It has come to my attention that there are many among you who do not know that healing on a spiritual level is available to everyone. We have been focused on healing the planet and healing our connection to one another, but these healings cannot come to fruition unless we heal or start to heal ourselves.

Many of the lightworkers question their reason for being here asking, "What is my mission in this lifetime?" I am here today to tell you the main mission of all humankind is to bring healing. The knowledge of how to heal is coded into your cell memory and your soul memory. If you are struggling with this concept there are healers among you who have remembered this ancient knowledge and are here to lead others to their awakening on how to heal yourself.

This healing begins with loving yourself enough to claim your right as a sovereign being to be healed of all physical, emotional, and spiritual trauma. It is your right to be gentle and forgiving with yourself, and it is your right to claim the powers that you have within to live a life not burdened by past trauma. Now is the time of the great awakening and along with this awakening comes great healing for all involved. Healing yourself and healing your family line will heal the world.

Isis, the Great Healer

AFFIRMATION

I claim my birthright to bring my mission of healing forth for everyone's benefit.

Fire Goddess

The Red Goddess of this land bids you welcome.

She is so pleased with the level of love and respect that she sees. Not only for the land and its sacredness but for each other. The daughters of the Goddess who have been called here at this time are so blessed with unlimited gifts and abilities. Each one of you holds a special place in bringing the Golden Age for this planet.

Do not ever get discouraged or question why you are here. At times, you may forget, but your soul will always bring you back to remembering. Just sit in silence and listen to the voice within. You have done this work in many lifetimes. You know what to do and how to do it. Among you there are teachers, healers, mystics, star beings, and earth anchors, but together you bring unlimited power here. You have unleashed a flow of love and healing. Each and every person who enters this land after you will feel this elevated energy. You bring the gift of renewal to all those who seek it with an open heart.

I am so proud of you, my daughters. I will be with you in Spirit wherever your travels take you to spread your message of love, light, and healing. Always choose from a place of love, and the love you seek will be magnified back to you.

I am Goddess, You Are Goddess, we are one! Go in love and spread the word *Kam ba la*, The anointed one in love.

AFFIRMATION

I am a part of something greater than myself and my uniqueness is a sacred contribution.

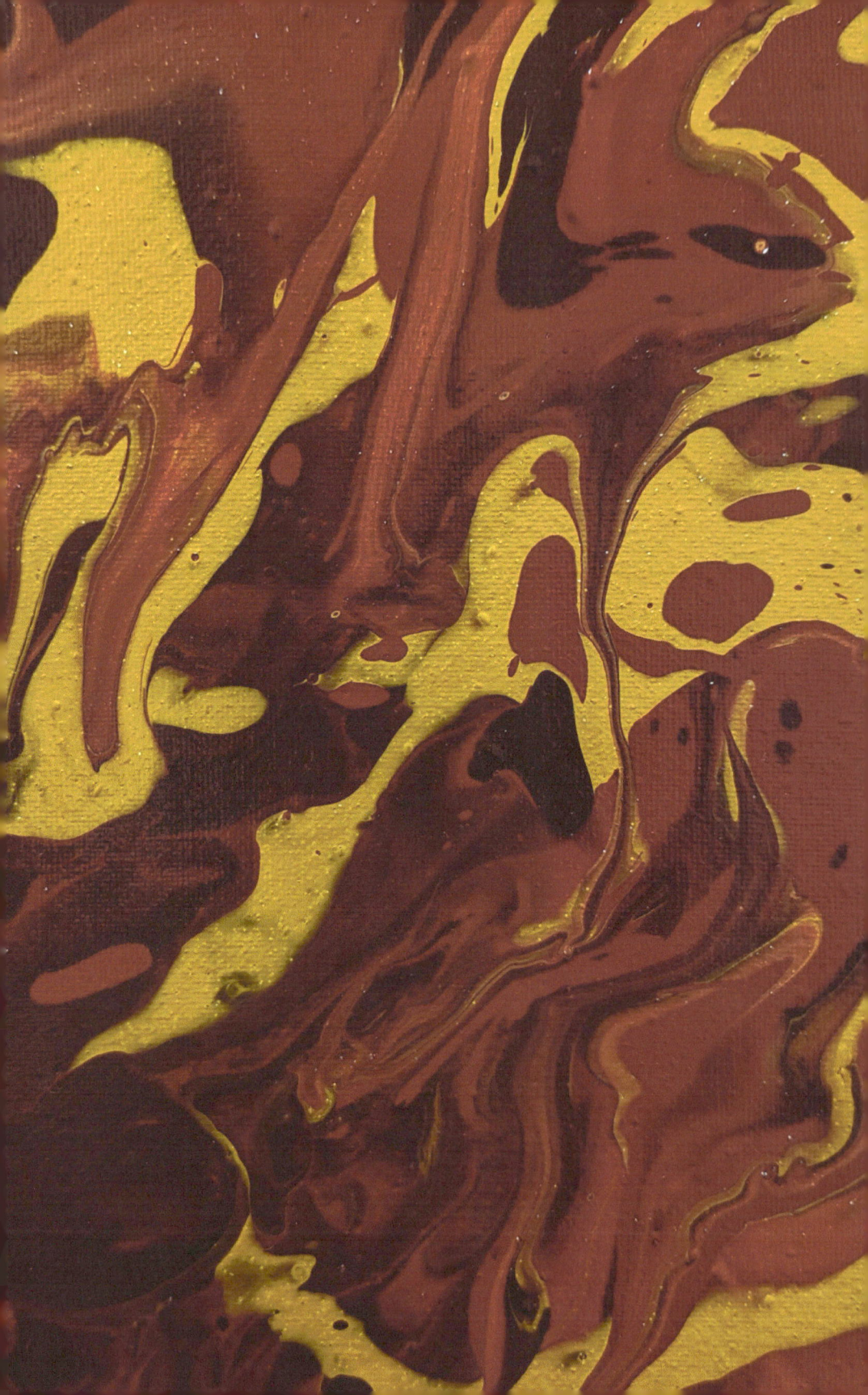

Isis

Welcome my beautiful daughters.

Many of you know in your soul that you have come home. The others will feel it, too, once the layers of remembering are pulled away. I am the Great Mother. I am your mother no matter what land you come from. Each of you is a beautiful creation from my womb. Open your hearts, your minds, and your bodies in order to receive the bountiful gifts I wish to impart upon you. Each and everyone of you are an unlimited being of Divine light and love. It is time to bring forth the Divine Feminine, no longer hiding it for fear of what others will think of you. I am your protector and will not allow anything or anyone to harm you.

You were all brought here together for a Divine appointment. You are my daughters who are anchoring the energy in this land for all daughters of the Divine that follow in your footsteps. This appointment is to be met with an open heart full of joy and bliss. It is not to be seen as an obligation or something too serious. Meet it with lightness, joy, and laughter and you will raise the vibration for the whole world. My gift to you, dear ones, is my love, my light, and my life. I am with you always. Go forth and shine!

AFFIRMATION

I am a beautiful creation from the womb of the Goddess.

Water Goddess

The Goddess of the creek spoke to me.

She is the ultimate example of renewal. She is constantly changing. She is never the same, second by second. Her waters are always flowing, always different, and always beautiful. She invites you to immerse yourself in her healing, loving waters. All are welcome here. This is a place of peace and serenity. Lay down your burdens and I will carry them away. Find rest and rejuvenation here.

My waters have been around this world and through each and everyone of you. There is no end to my waters, just like there is no end to you. We all continue to learn and grow and flow, coming back together again and again. Take your fill of all you need; there is plenty for everyone. No one will be denied the lifeblood of this beautiful planet. Refresh yourself, renew yourself, and always come back for more. We are all limitless, each in our own way. Take me in and take me with you. May we always flow as one.

AFFIRMATION

I am ever-changing and ever-flowing, just like the waters of the earth.

The Goddess Council

Our messages of late have been with a gentle reminder to take care of yourself and rise above the chaos and drama of your world.

Also, we have cautioned you to not take on the emotions, burdens, and drama of the people around you. The best way to counterbalance these lower vibrations surrounding you is to find your joy and happiness. You and only you are in control of your emotions and how you react to things. You are not to be drawn into other problems to solve. Show them by example. Show them that your life may not be perfect, but you choose to see the joy and beauty that is your life. Joy and happiness is the product of gratitude. The more you are grateful for all that is in your life, the more joy, happiness, and fulfillment you will feel. The beauty in this equation is the tremendous possibility of a life filled to overflowing with positive feelings and vibrations. The truly awakened beings know that the joy and happiness they feel is an inside job; no one can create it but themselves.

These messages are such a simple idea and not difficult to put into practice. We encourage you to start your day in a place of gratitude and the joy will flow freely to you. When people see your joy, the ones who are truly seeking will want to know how you have achieved it. This will be your opportunity to share this message with them. Sharing how you found your joy and happiness is one of simplest things you can do to keep the cycle of high vibration flowing in your life. No one said you have to be perfect before you can be happy and joyful. It is the Souls who have walked through fire in this life and choose to come out of it a better person who are the ones who truly understand the meaning of joy and happiness.

AFFIRMATION

My attitude of gratitude creates joy and happiness in my life.

Alleahel Star Being

I have shown up in your life to bring you wisdom from an ancient star.

We are beings from another solar system, and our forms are not solid like yours. I come from a planet that has mastered the art of living in peace and harmony. This is what I wish to impart on you. Regardless of the chaos that is surrounding you and your planet, you can create your own peace and harmony. It starts from within. Tap into your own Divine energy, that each and everyone of you have had with you since your inception. This Divine energy is where you will find the answers to living a fulfilled life. Each step you take to creating this life will bring more peace and harmony with it.

It is all in the Divine blueprint encoded in each and every one of your cells. All you have to do to access it is quiet the mind and open your Soul. Your Soul is longing for its original Divine plan and will welcome the steps needed to achieve your purpose for being here. Do not listen to anyone trying to tell you how you have to complete your mission. You and your team in Spirit are the only ones who know your life path. Follow the coding and your path will be opened to you.

The gift I bestow upon you is the gift of knowing. It has been there all along. I just created a quickening in your Spirit by my appearance. Now it is your turn to take this remembering and create your life of peace and harmony. Remember, as you do it for one of you, you do it for all of you. Do not lose heart—peace and harmony are part of your birthright and part of the Divine blueprint. Open yourself to what is already there!

AFFIRMATION

I open my divine blueprint and activate peace and harmony in my life.

Isis

My Beloveds, this is a message of forgiveness and release.

Forgiveness is a word with multi-layer meanings. Most people would automatically think of this word in relation to others. Today I want you to focus on this word in relationship to yourself. I want you to embrace this word. Practicing forgiveness sets you free. So let's start by forgiving yourself. Let go and release any choices from your past that you have not forgiven yourself for. You made these decisions to the best of your ability at the time. Even if you knew you were going against your inner knowing, it still was a lesson to pay more attention to what your body was telling you. It is also important in the forgiveness process to release others' expectations of who you should be. Your Soul knows who you should be and if that is not in alignment with others' expectations, that is their lesson to learn.

Self-forgiveness is learning to love every part of yourself. When you can accept who you are right now and who you are becoming, it takes your soul to a whole new level. When you release the unforgiveness that does not serve your higher purpose, you open yourself up to more knowledge, freedom, and love. It is important to forgive others on this path of reclaiming your higher self. It does not release them from the wrong; it releases you of the burden of carrying it around with you. This is where you can forgive others for not living up to your expectations. We all do it, but recognizing it starts the journey of releasing it.

My beloveds, I know you are spiritual beings living a human existence and it is easier to forgive sometimes and some people. Just remember it is all a part of your learning and growing. True spiritual connection requires you to face many difficulties as you evolve your Soul, but do not add suffering to these difficulties. Claim your right to live in love and harmony as you connect to your true purpose and a life well lived. End the suffering for yourself and others. Forgive yourself, love yourself and usher in a new world where all can thrive.

Your loving Mother

AFFIRMATION

I set myself free through forgiveness of myself and others.

Mary Magdalene

My dear child, do not let your heart be heavy by the burdens of your world.

You have the strength and abilities to conquer anything that is placed in your path. Obstacles are just temporary roadblocks to your destination. Do not let them stop you from creating the life you want. Reach deep down to your inner knowing. You will find the answers you seek. It is okay to know when you need help with something in your life. It is also perfectly okay to reach out and ask for help. This is not a sign of weakness. This is a sign of your ability to let go of control and receive help from another.

You are not meant to transverse this journey of life alone. The interconnectedness of others is the core reason you desire relationships. Open yourself up to receive help along your path, and you will build new relationships along the way. The Spirits around you cannot intervene with your free will, but they can orchestrate unbelievable abilities for you to meet the right person you need in your life at the right time. That is why you may think you have just stumbled upon the right spiritual teacher or a group of like-minded people. We are working in the background to bring you in contact with the people you need in your life. However, what you do with this meeting is up to you. We cannot make you choose to interact with them, but we can give you a gentle nudge in the right direction.

All of this message is to bring you the peace to know you are not alone in your life or spiritual journey. There are helpers all around you; those in human form and those in spirit form. Do not be afraid to accept help. You are one of the first ones to offer help. It is okay to receive and it is a blessing for the giver. Stay strong, my children, you are doing a fantastic job of creating your best life and evolving your spiritual life. I am here for you always.

AFFIRMATION

I am open to receiving help from others for my highest good.

Isis

Do not despair, my dear ones.

The world may seem in turmoil but there are many more peacekeepers that you never hear about. Unfortunately, there will always be times of trouble upon this earth. Not everyone chooses from a place of love. Many choose from a place of selfishness.

This war will not be the end of humanity or the world. However, it may be the end of an unsettled peace for a while. Long enough for those involved to learn their lessons or leave this earth plane. The Spiritual forces surrounding this planet are much greater than any forces upon the earth. We will do all in our power to see that their weapons fail.

Stay in a place of peace and love. Remember that only love is the greatest force and it will prevail. Do your part, continue to pray, and send healing energy into those areas that are affected. Visualize an army of Angels surrounding your planet. Do not give in to the fear that your media spreads. Remember, it is more about sensationalizing for the almighty dollar.

Come together in any way you can, be it in small groups or large. This is where the power is. The power of peace, love, and understanding will heal the world.

Isis, The Great Healer

AFFIRMATION

I am the power of peace, love and understanding that will heal the world.

Melchizedek

This is a day of magnificent energies.

Each person on this planet has the ability to call in and activate these energies. The energy of Source is unlimited. Once again, I have to remind you that you are the only one who puts limits on Source. As each individual steps up to claim their power, you will see a rise in the frequencies that can be measured. This is not a trick or a mistake. This is the belief in a higher power and in humanity's ability to claim their Divine right.

You will be hearing more and more about the Flower of Life and sacred geometry. If each lightworker that is anchoring the light was connected by lines, you would see the Flower of Life being created over the entire planet. This grid is being created to protect the earth and the beauty that is already here. The more the lightworkers become part of this grid, the more the dark cannot survive within the light.

Keep your light shining and know you are not alone. The team of angels, masters, guides, loved ones, and ancestors who want you to succeed is unlimited—and so is your power.

AFFIRMATION

I know the energy from Source is unlimited.

The Guardians of the Elements

The Guardians of the elements are always with you.

The Guardians of the Elements are just waiting to be called upon to lend their guidance and support. The Guardian of Earth watches over the planet ensuring we do not destroy what we have been given. The Guardian of Earth will also watch over you, helping to create a solid foundation in your life. The Guardian of Air is always surrounding you. We take air and breathing for granted, but the Guardian of Air ensures that our air is pure. The Guardian of Fire is just waiting for you to find your passion. Call upon the Guardian of Fire to fuel the areas of your life that are lacking energy and fire. The Guardian of Fire will give you the passion you need to succeed. The Guardian of Water is constantly flowing to you; just reach out your hand and receive the purifying energy of the Guardian of Water. Your Soul will be washed clean of any stagnant energy.

Each Guardian is special in their own right, but when calling on all four at once, they are a force that cannot be denied or stopped. They are just waiting to bring this energy to your life so you can succeed in your mission.

AFFIRMATION

I call upon The Guardians for support in all areas of my life.

The Goddess Council

Your life is ever flowing like the waters of this earth.

Each one is a precious commodity and a limited resource. What you do with your life can leave a lasting mark on this earth. What you do with the water that has been given to you to use will also show how well it has been cared for.

The Goddesses are with you today and everyday. We are encouraging you to elevate your life and live as pure as you want your water to be. Do not fill your body with foods that don't nourish it. Don't fill your head with ideas that do not serve you or the greater good. Now is the time to tune into your own intuition on a soul level. You have the answers you seek. If you are not sure, feel into how the idea sits with your body. Do you feel expansion or contraction? Expansion encourages you to move forward with your ideas. Your life will flow like the waters of the earth. Ever-changing, ever-growing, ever-knowing.

AFFIRMATION

I flow with the expansions of my life.

Council of 12

This is a message of boundless energy.

We limit ourselves by believing there is not enough to go around. We are here to tell you there is enough for everyone and more. Think of the energy of a child. They know no limits until their parents tell them there are. We want you to live your life like there are no limits. We are not talking about excess in the material world. We are talking about your potential in your senses in the psychic realm.

You can be a conduit for Spirit. Just open and allow. Do not be afraid. If you are living a life of alignment with spiritual connection and high vibration, nothing can harm you from this world or the spirit world. The bumps in the road map of your life are to teach you to have faith in yourself and your abilities. You are your greatest resource. You have unlimited energy and potential. Have faith in yourself and your choices.

We are all here waiting for you to open up to our guidance. We will not make the choices for you, but we will help you see what is for your highest and best. Do not wander this journey called life alone; tap into the endless energy of the Universe. You are a magnificent being of love, light, and potential.

AFFIRMATION

The energy of the Universe is endless and available to me.

Isis

Lay down your burdens at my feet.

You are not meant to travel this journey alone. You are not meant to carry everyone else's burdens. Take heart, dear one, for yours is a special mission. It is a mission of love and laughter. How can you perform your mission if you carry the weight of the world upon your shoulders? Release that which is not yours; surround yourself with protection. Call upon the Angels to protect you, if you cannot hold that space for yourself. Do not forget to clear your energy and your space. Once again, you cannot fulfill your mission if your energy is constantly being drained by others. Create your sacred space, and put up your boundaries energetically and physically. It is not selfish. In the long run, it will serve the greater good if you serve yourself first.

Remember you are a part of the Goddess and you deserve the same reverence and treatment that you afford the Goddess. Embrace yourself, love yourself, and above all, value yourself as the precious life that you are. The Goddess within and the Goddess without is bound to no one. Honor your commitment to yourself by taking care of you. Then everyone in your life will benefit from the love and joy you radiate.

AFFIRMATION

I release the weight of the world from my shoulders and step into my life's mission.

The Galactic Council

The energies that are reaching you and the earth at this time are Galactic.

There are beings beyond your five senses that have been sent here to prevent a major catastrophic event. Your world will no longer be allowed to destroy itself through wars and advanced technologies. There are too many enlightened Souls populating the earth at this time to allow this to happen.

We are working in tandem with these Souls to raise the vibration of mankind. Most, not all, will no longer follow false leaders. Their Souls are aware of what the world of the Golden Age feels like. They will continue to move forward to create another Golden Age upon earth by merging the new world and what they remember of their old world through past life memories.

The Galactic Council has been watching from afar for too long. It is now apparent that we need to reside alongside you to bring about this Golden Age. Just as a parent walks beside a child holding its hand and guiding them, we will do the same. There is so much knowledge being downloaded at this time to the beings who are aligned with the energies of the greater good and the Universal connectedness. Each individual with these gifts will continue to share, heal, and live a life of love and joy.

Each time you share your many gifts with the world, you are one step closer to creating this Golden Age. All are invited to participate in creating and connecting to this world. It all comes down to a matter of choice. Choose a life in service to the enlightened ones and you will receive your share in this magnificent age. You cannot outgive what the Universal forces are waiting to present to you. Continue to live your life in love and connectedness.

AFFIRMATION

I choose to share my gifts to make our world a better place to live.

Team in Spirit

Heed the words of the Goddess.

Do not worry and do not fear. Place your cares at our feet. We are here to lift you up to be our voice to all who will listen. Do not cloud your thoughts with negativity; this only crowds out the good. All is well in your world and unfolding just as it should be. You have been protected in so many ways in this lifetime and this is just another example. Do not fret; you have absolute abundance for this.

There is healing going on behind the scenes. Just let go of the form and know the Creator/Creatrix has this. It will manifest beyond your wildest dreams. Enjoy this time and this bonding and know that each of you are important to your mission.

AFFIRMATION

I have healthy relationships in my life that support my mission.

Element of Air

The Element of Air is a powerful force today.

This is a gentle reminder to not forget the power in all the elements. They are life sustainers, but if not respected, they can diminish a life. There is no end to the call to action to take care of what you have been given. Too many people assume it will always be there. I am here today to remind you that your time upon this planet is very short, compared to how long the elements have been around. However, it is still very important that you respect them for their life-giving qualities. Just like all Souls are connected to each other, every element is connected to those same Souls. They are also connected to every living thing upon this earth.

This is a gentle warning to come into alignment with the elements and your fellow man. It is not too late. Earth has the amazing ability to regenerate itself. So does each and every human on this planet. Take a lesson from nature. Beautify your space, respect others, and work together to create a life of balance and harmony. Do these things and you will see a life full of promise and beauty. Do it out of love and not duty. This is what is needed to make this world continue for generations to come. What better gift can you give your children and grandchildren than a beautiful planet earth?

AFFIRMATION

I am in alignment with the elements and with all of humankind.

Master Guide

Enough time has passed.

You have stalled long enough. It is time for you to get about the business of spreading the messages of love and light to the world. Do not be afraid to be seen or heard. We will be with you guiding your way and giving you the added courage you need. Now is the time to take the action steps.

Do what it takes in your world. Be fearless! You cannot hide forever behind the mundane. Your pull to complete your mission is too great. You are only prolonging what is meant for you! There are beings greater than you working behind the scenes—just trust them!

AFFIRMATION

I am spreading the message of love and light to the world.

The Law of Love and Oneness

This is only a message of love and connection.

Now is the time to truly embrace your brothers and sisters. We are all one. Release any judgment; open your heart to give and receive love. When all is said and done in your short time on this planet, only love is real. We may take our memories with us to the next lifetime, but the love we give and receive is what truly elevates the soul.

This is the simplest explanation, yet the hardest thing to accomplish. Love everyone where they are. It is not your job to figure it out for them. They have their own journey—a journey that is a lifetime of learning and growing. Recognize and honor the Spark of the Divine in all living things.

AFFIRMATION

The love I give and receive elevates my Soul.

Council of 12

Do not be deceived by illusions.

All is not as it appears. Be present in the moment and watchful to what is going on around you. Do not rush forward in either direction. Bide your time, for the truth will be revealed. You are Divinely protected and directed. Make all decisions from a place of truth and integrity. When you come from a place of love and kindness, all will be well. The pain will pass and you will open yourself up to wonderful new experiences.

You did not get to this point through an illusion, everything you saw and felt is very real. Accept what is. Do not try to make it something it is not or can't be. All will be well for all involved. Just remember to speak your truth with kindness.

It will be obvious very soon what direction this is headed. Do not find fault. Thank that which you have received and release that which no longer serves you. We are with you always, offering support and love. Just remember strength in all things.

AFFIRMATION

I am Divinely protected as I make my decision from a place of truth and integrity.

Ascended Masters

This message is coming from the Masters.

We are a group of higher Souls who have lived many incarnations on earth and have gathered an unlimited abundance of knowledge. This is what we want to say to you today. Do not limit yourself by the small definition of abundance. It is so much more than your money and your things. Abundance of knowledge and learning is something that you take with you for each of your lifetimes. Abundance of family and friends is something you can enjoy right now, but they also go with you in Soul groups for many lifetimes.

The most important of all is the abundance of love. Love yourself, love your fellow man, and love your planet. Even if you don't know what to do to make your world better, just remember love makes everything better. Send it out in waves every day. Send it out to all who will embrace and accept love even if they do not know where it is coming from. We have been sending you many messages of love, for it is the only way to claim the Golden Age that was promised to your earth.

Within the vibration of love, there is a code that will open the doors to a better life. This vibration is so high that the lower vibration emotions cannot be sustained when it is released. The more people who call upon the vibration of love and light, the faster the darkness will disappear.

This is an urgent message to all lightworkers and we will keep sending it forth until it is rooted in your deepest psyche and shared on your every breath. Remember, you are all shielded in a cocoon of love and light and there is enough for everyone. Please share it and spread it to all the corners of your world. We will all benefit from this movement.

AFFIRMATION

My life is abundant in all areas, especially love.

Ancestors of the Land

We are the ancestors of this land.

Please heed the message of the Spirits of the land. We did not, and now we are trying to rectify that which we have done. It is through the generations that keep returning to purify and cleanse that which we abused.

If you are called to the land, you are a soul of us that has been purified by fire and will love and respect the land, not position and power. There have been many civilizations that have fallen into corruption and greed. Those are no longer walking upon the earth. You have the heart and the abilities to succeed where we have failed. Keep spreading the message of love and respect for this life-giving land. All who honor and respect her will be blessed. We know you can achieve this.

AFFIRMATION

I will love and respect the beauty of the land.

The Galactic Council

The energy of love, light, and change is available to all today.

The portal is wide open and just waiting for you to step through it. Release the fear and uncertainty around your growth potential and your abilities. We are here to tell you that you have unlimited potential. It is only you who keeps you from reaching new heights.

The 5-5-5 portal is a moment in time when all the worlds and all beings have the greatest potential for change and connection. Connect with other beings, connect to the earth, and connect with each other. Sometimes the greatest growth and change comes from our connection with others. Have you ever been struggling with an issue and suddenly you meet someone who is going through or has been through the same thing? This is not a coincidence. This is divinely orchestrated to aid in your growth, understanding, and love.

Use this 5-5-5 portal to get clear on what you want your life to look and feel like. Connect with these energies that make the impossible possible. Purify your heart and your body and be open to receive all that is yours. This is your lifetime to claim your sovereignty and the ability to live it. We are always watching and encouraging you.

AFFIRMATION

I use the energy of numbers to create my life and connect to others.

Element of Air

The Element of Air is answering my call today.

A strong wind is blowing from the East. It is showing up today to cleanse and purify my body, mind, and soul from all that does not serve my highest good.

The strong wind is reminding me to be flexible. Bend with the winds of change and you will not break. The air is also reminding me to take deep cleansing breaths. Breathe in the life force energy of air and breathe out all your worries.

The breath of life flows through each and everyone of us. It is just another element that proves we are all connected. On your next breath, send out love and light to all who will embrace it and it will return to you tenfold. The elements love and respect you and all they ask is for you to do the same. Take a deep breath and blow your dreams and wishes into the air.

AFFIRMATION

I breathe in life-force energy, and I breathe out what no longer serves me.

Spirit of the Land

I am blessed to be in this land.

I am blessed to be of the land. I am welcomed as one of us. You have the love and respect of our land. All who gaze upon the land with reverence and awe will always be welcome on this island. We invite you of the highest vibration to share your energy with us.

Please encourage all who come here to walk upon the land with curiosity and respect. We, the Spirits of this land, will not hesitate to protect all we can. We do not wish harm upon anyone, but we will do what we must to preserve what is left of Mu. When the people upon the land do not show proper respect, they will be spewed out just like your ancestors. We mean no harm. We are a lover of all life, but we are the guardians of the land and to that, we owe our deepest devotion.

Do not take this as a warning, but as a request. There are many among you who are all about the love of this Earth. It is to you that we ask to please educate and encourage others to embrace the life-giving force of this land and in return, you will continue to receive all that this land has to give.

Mahola

AFFIRMATION

I will share my love of the land with all who hear my voice.

Goddess of Fire

Goddess of the South and fire, I am here with you today to encourage you to find your passion and excitement.

Burn brightly so all will want to know where your secret fire comes from. Not a fire to consume but a fire to illuminate the darkness and show others the way to a life filled with energy and passion. Do not let anyone or anything dim your fire. You are a unique being of light. A Way-shower for all those lost in darkness. Do not fear the unknown, for your fire and your light will dispel any low vibrations you come up against. There is no darkness your light cannot penetrate. Your fire and passion are a creative force. Use it to create the life you are meant to live, and the love you are meant to give.

AFFIRMATION

I burn with the passion of creativity.

Sekhmet

Daughters of Isis and sisters of the heart.

I bid you welcome to the sacred land. You have all walked this path before, and you will all walk it again. There are many healers among you, not just of the body, but of the heart. Each time you heal yourself, one of your sisters, or one of your brothers, you are bringing healing to this earth. It is not for the faint of heart, but initiation never is. Each time you embrace a challenge in your life and learn and grow from it, you are up-leveling your Soul.

Be sure to nourish your body, mind, and spirit whenever you feel the need. The Goddess wants you whole and healthy. Your mission is to take care of yourself first and set an example for others. How can you teach, how can you give what you do not know or do for yourself? Relish your time in this sacred land and the abundant love I feel radiating out of each and every one of you. Our power to give to you is limitless. All you have to do is ask and receive. Just as we have asked you to come to the land and receive the gifts we wish to impart on you.

Be the enlightened one, be the beloved one, and be a spiritual beacon whose light is never diminished or depleted. Rest and rejuvenate in the loving arms of the mother.

AFFIRMATION

I nourish my body, mind, and spirit creating wholeness for me and the world.

The Goddess Council

Set your focus on the beautiful earth all around you.

Seek your peace in nature. Let go of the visions of a man-made life. Material possessions are not the answer. When you turn to Mother Earth to fill your life with beautiful things, you will never be disappointed. If you focus on the havoc and chaos around you, you will not achieve the peace you seek.

Spend as much time in nature as possible. Spend time with loved ones and friends who raise your vibration. The higher you vibrate, the more in tune you will be with Mother Earth.

Respect all living creatures, plants, animals, and other humans. Even if you don't see it, everything has a soul or what we call an inner Spirit. Honor the Spirit in everything. When you live from a place of love you will receive the peace that you seek. Peace is the achievement of love. We cannot express enough how important love for everything is. Love is what will raise the vibration of the whole earth and create peace for all. Love can achieve miracles and save mankind.

Spread the love like it's your last day on this plane and you will be granted many years to accomplish your goals.

AFFIRMATION

The time I spend in nature replenishes my Soul.

The Galactic Council

This is a day of tremendous energy and power.

This is a day of new beginnings and starting on the next adventure of your life. Everything you have experienced is preparing you for the next shift that will require a lot of energy and fortitude. You are being called upon to not only anchor the energy of a new age, but to spread the word of the new age.

There are many sharers and there are many seekers out there. You do not have to choose which one you are. You can be both. Once you have gained knowledge by seeking, you can then share this knowledge with others. You are living in a world full of wonders and miracles. Be the light that draws these into your life. The more you receive, the more you have to give. Share all the simple wonders of your life. It does not have to be a grand gesture. It only has to be heart-centered.

Stand up today and claim the energies that are being sent to every corner of your planet. Sometimes it is hard to understand what one small thing can accomplish, but we see the bigger picture. The more you seek spiritual knowledge, the better this world will be for everyone. The high vibration pulsating through your body is like a beacon of light. It attracts more high-vibration energy and people. Accept that you are a part of a greater plan to raise the vibrations of the planet and save mankind.

AFFIRMATION

I am a receiver of knowledge and I share my knowledge with the world.

Isis

Dear Ones! It is with great honor that I welcome you here tonight.

A night of magic, of wonders, and of awesome power. Each one of you has been selected to be here. No matter how you think it came about, it was orchestrated by me. I am so pleased with the level of your vibrations. You are a beacon for this world. Each one of you is here today with special gifts and abilities. I am here to tell you to accept these gifts. Welcome them into your life and share them with your world. You do a great service for mankind, by anchoring in the energy of love and light. Do not fear the darkness even though at times it feels immense. The light is beginning to overtake it and it starts with each of you.

You amplify the power of the God and Goddess. You embody the God and Goddess. You are the God and Goddess. I may speak to you like you are one of my children, but in reality I speak to you in the loving voice of a mother. You are a part of me and we all need that loving voice telling us that we are amazing creatures without any boundaries or limitations. So, my dear ones, reach for the stars. Manifest the life of your dreams. You are worthy to receive this and so much more. Keep shining your light, keep loving your fellow man, and keep being you.

AFFIRMATION

I have been blessed with special gifts and abilities.

Team in Spirit

Heed the words of the Goddess.

You cannot fully commit to your mission if you are always coming to someone else's rescue. I know this sounds counter to your mission, but every time you are dragged into someone else's personal drama, your attention is taken away from getting your message out for the greater good.

That does not mean to totally step away from your loved ones, but be aware of your boundaries and when it is your choice to help them. You cannot always be their dumping ground. It is not your responsibility to come up with answers for all their problems. You have had enough of your own problems in this lifetime and you have walked through fire and come out transformed on the other side.

You must let someone else experience this for themselves. If they do not learn from their experiences, it is their choice. You cannot make the blind see, the deaf hear, or the sick heal unless they want it for themselves. This is a freeing concept that gives you permission to be and choose for you. We are lovingly supporting you through everything you are going through. We are here today to tell you that you deserve the peace and freedom you seek. Do not let anyone or anything take that away from you. It is your birthright.

Read these words over and over again whenever you are pulled into someone else's drama. We will do all in our power to keep you safe, protected, and heading in the right direction.

AFFIRMATION

I have healthy boundaries for myself and with others.

Spirit Guides

Do not dwell on the past.

You did everything in your power to make things good. This is not your lesson, so release any guilt or doubt. You need to make this decision for yourself in order to learn your own life lesson. How can you learn to put yourself first if you are spending all your energy fulfilling someone else's needs?

Your time of mothering has come to an end. Now is the time to bring forth the Goddess. Make your choices and decisions based on what a Goddess would choose. She would never accept someone treating her less than another; why should you accept treating yourself this way?

You are a radiant being of light. Once you accept this and start treating yourself this way, you will draw people into your life who see you as a Goddess and treat you as a Goddess. The love that surrounds you knows no bounds. Feel the embrace of all who came before you and all who will come after you. You are healing this for all of you. Your granddaughter will live to see this in her lifetime, the rise of the Goddess and the return of women to a true and respected place in society.

AFFIRMATION

I make decisions for my life that will elevate the Divine Feminine.

Master Guide

Your world is a wonderful place.

Lay down your fears and your worries; there is no foundation to these negative thoughts you are having. Be thankful for all that you have been given. You are well protected and you will not be left wanting. Do your best with what has been given to you, and you will continue to be blessed.

Blessings are an unlimited gift from God/Goddess. Keep your thoughts positive. You are living an amazing life in an amazing place. It is time to open your heart and home, and embrace the new people who are coming into your life. Do not fear your discernment, just go with your intuition. There is someone out there as unique as you. Have faith and hope—you will not be steered wrong.

AFFIRMATION

*I am grateful for the amazing life
I have been blessed with.*

Radiant Beings of Light

Children of the earth, now is a time of celebration.

Not for what you think it is for, but a celebration of the light over darkness. Celebrate your fellow man, encourage them to live a life of purpose and love. Do not judge, but support each other. The celebration of light is not limited by beliefs, all are welcome. There is no separation between beings. Each one has a Soul of pure love and light. The sooner people remember this, the sooner you will live in a world of peace and love.

Break down the barriers of all kinds. There is no race, there is no religion, and there is no gender. There is only pure love and light. Dear ones, I am of the light. These messages are to help you remember. Once you remember you are a Divine being, you will not need outside sources to make you whole. You have the power of creation within you. Whatever you think, you will create. Be sure to keep your thoughts only at the lightest level of love.

Love is the key to manifesting. Any other low-vibration emotions will derail you manifesting the life of your dreams. Thank the low-vibration emotions for the lessons they have brought to your life and send them on their way. The light shines greater than the brightest star.

AFFIRMATION

*I have the power of creation within me.
I create a life of love and light.*

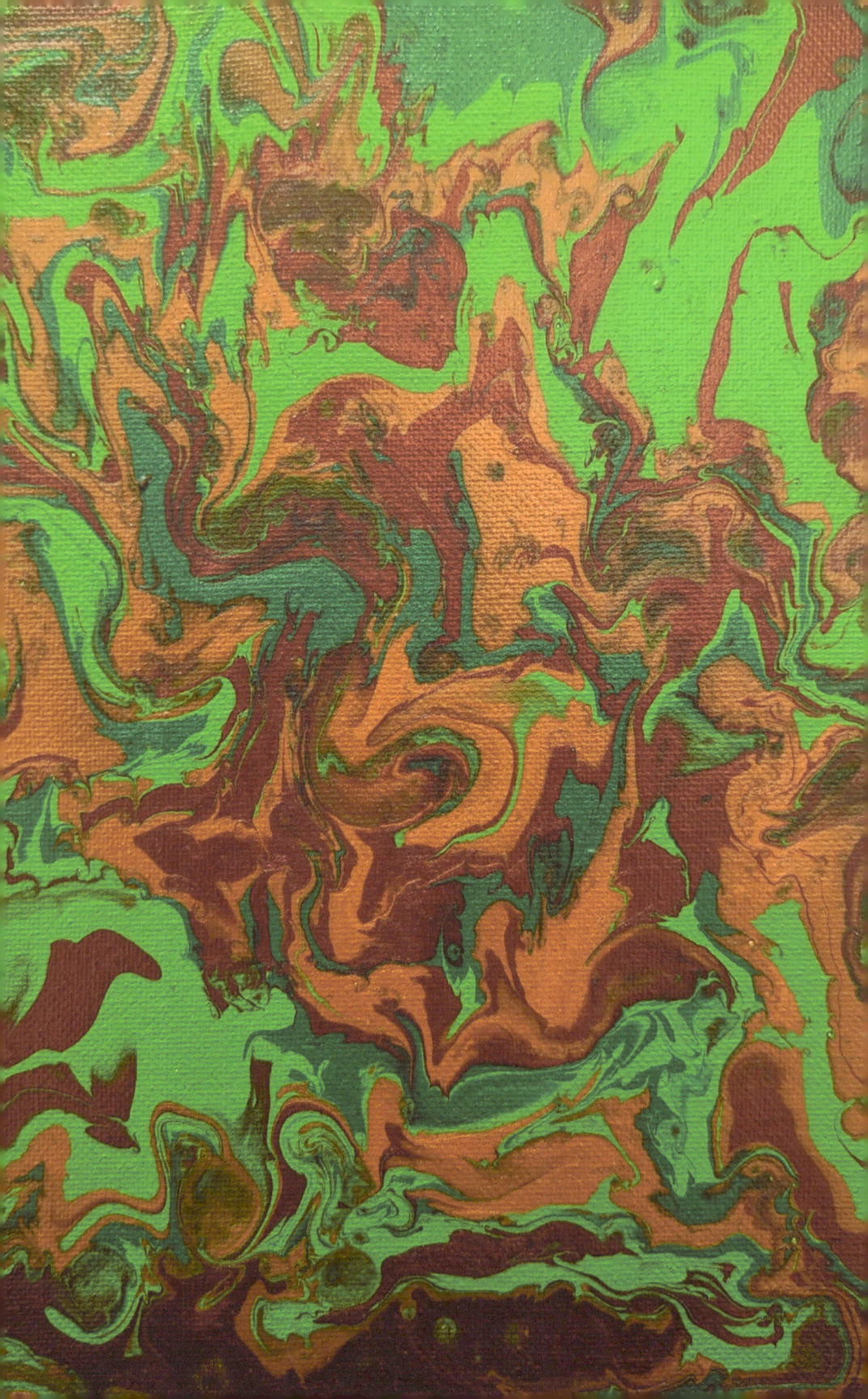

The Law of Numbers

The vibration of this 2 portal day is the vibration of coming together.

For too long, the people of the earth have been separated by the belief in individual independence. Now is the time to learn that you are all connected. What one person does affects many more people than they even know. 22222 is all about connection. Connect to the energy, connect to your fellow humans, and connect to this beautiful planet that provides for all your needs. When you learn this lesson of connection, you learn how important each and everyone of you are. There is no greater, there is no less, there is only balance.

This balance and respect is what will pull your world out of its destructive path. You are all equally important and are needed to make this world a better place. The breakdown is in the duality of two sides to everything; this is how your world is set up. There is the high-vibration side and the low-vibration side. The beauty in this is you get to decide what side you are choosing to live on. When you choose to love, respect and treat each other with kindness you are choosing the high-vibration way of life. You get this choice several times in your day.

The other energy of this day is the three. The energy of the 3 is all about communication. Communicating is the key to understanding each other. Open your lines of communication, and remove judgment and assumptions. Really get to know the people in your world. The basic truth beneath all your differences is you are all the same. You feel, you love, and you want a fulfilling life. Let's work together to make this a reality for everyone. Use the energy portal of today to make things happen. Share your love and your time with someone today and start the healing for all.

AFFIRMATION

I maintain my individuality as I unite with others for a common cause.

Dolphin Spirit

On this significant day of the power of two we come to you as a pair.

The dolphins are trying to spread the message of unity. We are better together than separate. There is no difference between us. We swim in the same waters, we eat the same foods, we feel the same way and we are all in this together. The sooner the human race acknowledges these ideas among themselves, the sooner they can come together to save this planet. It is not a free for all with everyone doing the taking. Soon there will be nothing left to take.

Use this powerful day of the two energies to come together. Make room for each other in your life, share what you have been blessed with, and love without judgment. We are all on this planet together and together we must protect and nurture what we have been given. This attitude and thought process is what will save the human race and this magnificent planet that we live on. It takes each of you to bring about a world of love and peace. Once it starts, it will spread to every corner of the planet, and it will benefit all who live here. Take pride in being a part of the race that save and preserved this living breathing planet.

AFFIRMATION

I work well with others to create a fulfilling life for everyone.

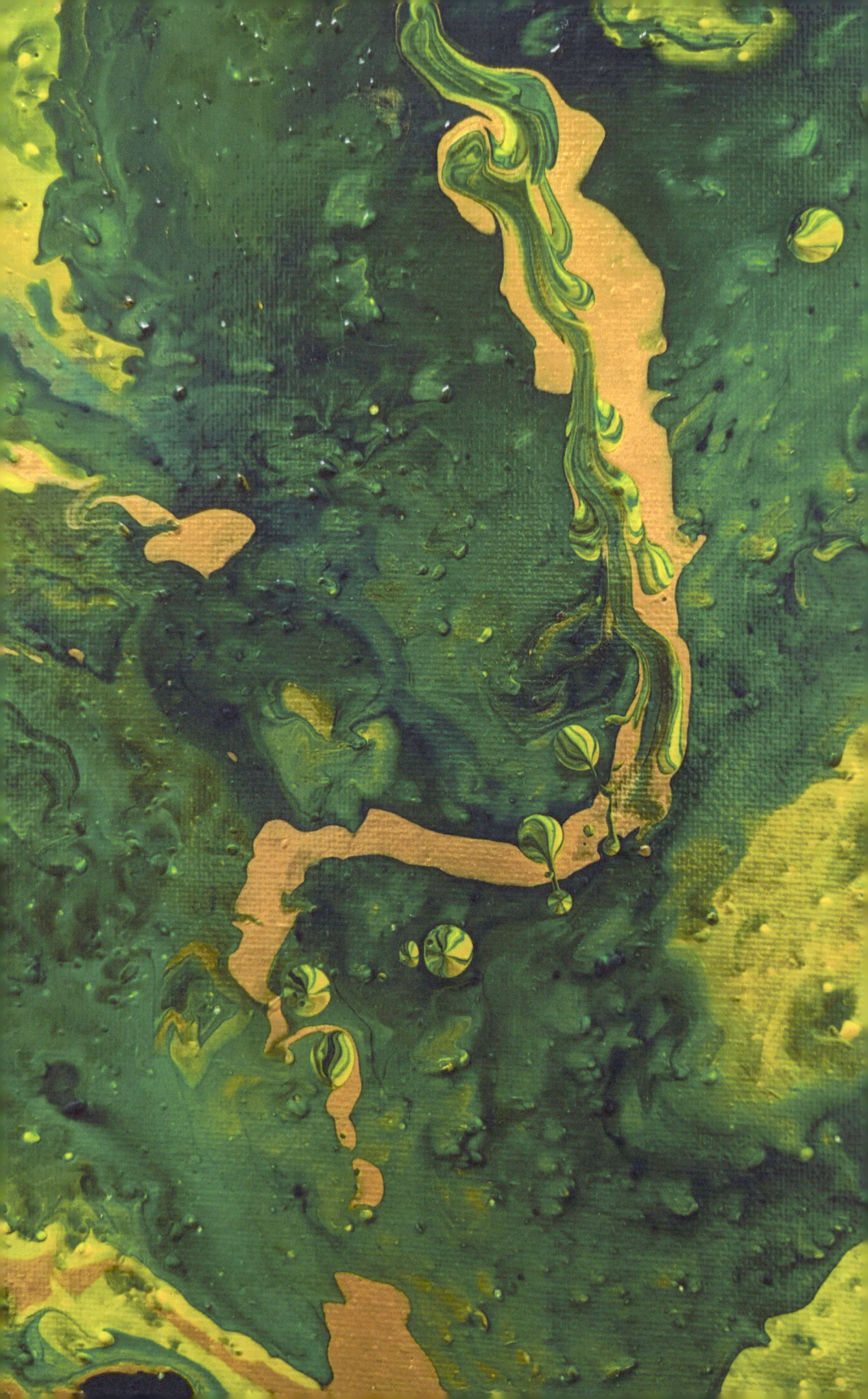

The Spirits of Love

Welcome home my dear child.

Home is where you are the happiest. It does not matter where in the world that is. It is wherever you feel the most comfortable in your own skin. It is so important at this period in time that you find the peace you seek from within. You cannot always control outside circumstances, but you can always control how you react to them.

I feel thoughts and energy swirling around like a whirlpool. We are here to reassure you that all will be well. Things in the world will calm down just to rise up again in another area. Your prayers of concern for your fellow humans have been heard. We are working toward a favorable outcome. However, there is still free agency in your world, and if a person does not choose from a place of love, we can only do our best to protect others in the path. Your world is not as bad as it seems. There is so much love and so much light. Unfortunately, only the darkness is highlighted. Do not fall victim to the gloom and doom that people are spouting. Focus on the love and relationships in your life. This is the reality of your world; the other is an illusion and illusions disappear as fast as they appear.

Stay strong, stay resilient, and stay in love! We are all here!

AFFIRMATION

I carry the peace and love of home within me wherever I go.

Father Tree

The Spirit of the trees bid you welcome to their land.

It is an honor to cradle you in our loving embrace. We are full of ancient knowledge and wisdom. We are so happy to share it with you. Please partake of what we have to offer. You may receive these gifts just by being in the land. If you want a more intimate experience, please feel free to hug us or sit among our roots. There are many among you who are already communicating with us. We love that.

For so long, we have stood as silent sentinel of this land, before your race started to move among us. We have suffered at the hands of some of your people, but the ones like yourselves that approach with loving reverence make up for it. We will continue to stand as watchers here. We are proud to shelter so many creatures among our branches and bark. We will continue to embrace the humans that come here for peace, love, and understanding.

We have all come from the same source, so even though we may look different than you, we are a part of you and you are a part of us. Keep spreading the love and protecting our planet in any way you can. Remember you have our welcome and our blessing as you move forward on your path bringing more love and light into the world.

AFFIRMATION

I honor the knowledge and wisdom of the trees and accept it gratefully.

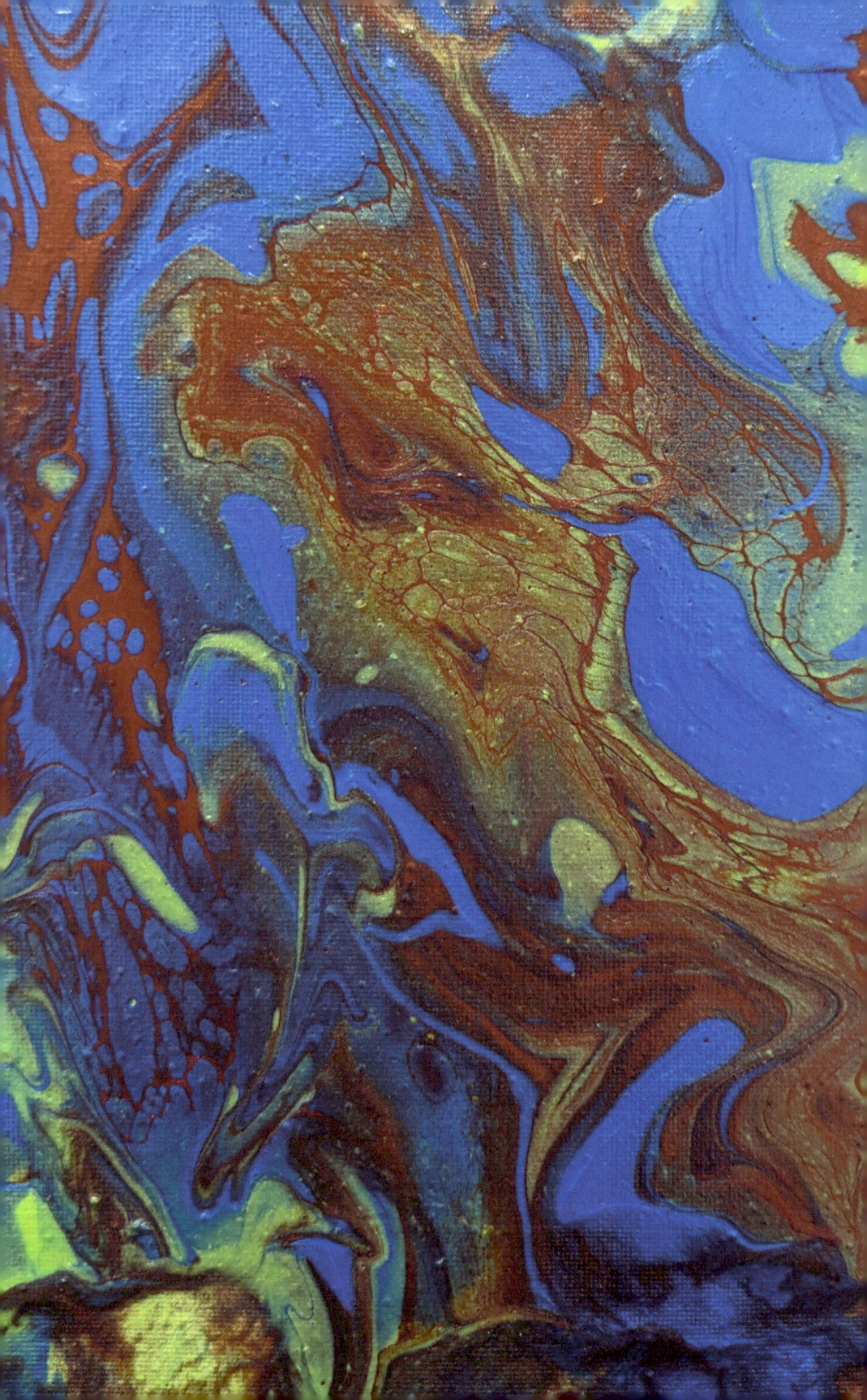

Spirit of Generosity

Be open to receiving.

Your path has not been an easy one, but you have learned so many lessons and conquered so many mountains. Now is the time to be open and receive. Your gifts are many, but there are even more waiting for you. We know you have a hard time asking for help or just receiving something from someone. At this time, we are asking you to be the gracious receiver. It is okay to let someone else be the giver. You allow them the pleasure of that position as long as they are giving from the heart.

There is so much here for you to receive from this land, from your instructors, and from your fellow sisters. Embrace each one and be open to what they offer you. There is so much love and generosity that no one will feel depleted. Be open, be whole, and be love.

AFFIRMATION

I am open to receive all the blessings from any and all sources.

Ancient Warrior Spirit

There is an ancient knowledge and wisdom that wishes to be heard.

These lands have heard and seen many things, some good and some bad, yet they continue to welcome the spirit of the humans. There is so much richness and nurturing they are here to offer if only you take the time to receive it. Sit upon the land and let your body sink into the soil. Release the tension from your muscles, release the thoughts from your mind, and just be. It is in the silence and the stillness that you will receive your greatest gift. The gifts do not have to be some spectacular feat; just the gift of being present and receiving is enough.

The ancients knew this. That is why in so many cultures they would venture into the woods to commune with nature. It was to absorb the knowledge and receive their wisdom. Every plant, every tree, every bird, and every animal had a lesson for them, even before what was imparted to them by the Great Spirit.

Just sit still in nature and open your heart. Listen from your heart and not your head. All your answers are there. Many think they cannot do this where they are, that they must make a pilgrimage to sacred land. All of this beautiful earth is sacred land and the beauty of that is it is everywhere for you. You only have to be still and receive.

AFFIRMATION

I have the gift of being still and present throughout my day.

Master Guide

Do not fear that you have made the wrong choice.

You have chosen from a place of love for all concerned. You have chosen from deep in your Soul, knowing that you have a mission upon this earth that requires a deeper connection to Spirit—a connection that cannot be maintained under constant stress, frustration, and anger.

Your mission requires you to come from a place of peace, love, and comfort. You are working toward that place of balance and harmony. You are so close and the Universe is working towards the same goal. Release any fears, guilt, or concerns; yours is a higher purpose and has no room for low-vibration emotions or beings. Do not take that statement in a superior way. It is just a confirmation that you are on the right path and headed in the right direction. A life of love, light, and laughter to be shared with all.

AFFIRMATION

The Universe is working with me and supporting me.

The Watchers

We are called The Watchers.

Our name has been used by many people and other groups. We are the group that have been watching over your planet since it has been inhabited by humans. We were assigned this task by the Creator of all that is. Our main function is to watch from afar to prevent humans from destroying all life upon your planet. There are many inhabited planets throughout the galaxies, and each one has a group of watchers. They can only intervene in dire circumstances. Our involvement is very remote in order for humans to learn on their own. They must realize that their planet is a beautiful place that will supply all of their needs if they lovingly take care of all they have been given.

There are miraculous cures to be found among the plants and animals. They must be treated with respect and reverence in order for them to give up their secrets. Too many animals and plants have chosen to leave this earth. Some because of the treatment by humans and some because they had served their purpose and they were moving on to other planets.

The Watchers are also observing the people on your planet who are striving to help their fellow man, the animals, and the environment. Each time an act of kindness is performed we see a green light pulsating out from the spot. It appears like a heartbeat. Whenever we see this outpouring of love, it gives us hope that mankind is really awakening to the true meaning of unconditional love. The love of all is the answer to all. May you be a source generating love and a receptor to receive love.

AFFIRMATION

My world is protected by Divine Beings.

The Law of Numbers

This is a day of infinite possibilities.

The 8/8 is often referred to as the Lion's Gate. We see it as a continuous circuit that can be used to manifest whatever you want to create in your life. The double eights are a sign from the Universe of unlimited abundance. Abundance comes in many forms. It does not just represent the material world. It applies to all areas of your life. There is abundant love, gratitude, and happiness.

The 8/8 on its side are two interlocking infinity signs. Use the power of this sacred geometry as a manifesting tool. Meditate upon this symbol and be open to the possibilities that show up in your life. Use this symbol to activate the energies within your own body. Imagine the figure eight or the infinity symbol surrounding you. It is used to clear blocks and activate your energy centers. There is unlimited life force energy waiting to fill you up, so you will never feel depleted again. Use the 8/8 symbol to bring people together in peace and harmony. Visualize it as a protection above and below your gathering. It will gather the energy from the cosmos and the energy from Mother Earth and bring a beautiful balance to all within this amazing container.

It is so important to look upon your life as a continuous flow of energy. Remember, you are constantly moving, changing, and evolving. Even when something may feel uncomfortable, remember it won't last long. This experience is adding to your growth and endless possibilities of who you may become. However you see this day, look upon it with openness and wonder and you will receive the gifts of infinite possibilities. We are all infinite beings that have no beginning and no end. We just are!

AFFIRMATION

I use the power of sacred geometry to manifest abundance in all areas of my life.

Isis

As the spiral of life continues to turn, so do your choices in life.

I am here today to encourage you to step boldly into your life. Do not choose from a place of fear or comfort. Choose from a place of experiencing all that life has to offer you; as a place of wonder and adventure, it will not disappoint you. It will deliver a life full of lessons that will elevate the Soul. The lessons do not have to be steeped in spiritual material to grow your soul. Some of the simplest things you experience on your earth plane create the largest expansion. A simple appreciation of a flower growing through the crack in a sidewalk is a lesson in tenacity and perseverance. The simple act of a smile or a greeting is spreading love and light.

For many of you humans talk about a grand mission during your time on this planet. I am here to tell you just the act of incarnating at this time and agreeing to experience the good and the bad is your grand mission. I feel like I keep repeating this message and I will keep repeating it until you understand. You are perfect on a soul level, you are enough and you are the light that will bring your world out of the darkness.

AFFIRMATION

I step boldly into the life of my choosing.

Spirit of the Wind

Now is a time of great change in your world and your life.

You have not come here to remain the same person throughout your whole life. You are designed to grow and evolve. You have been gifted with the abilities of reason and knowledge. Now is the time to use these skills to create whatever you want in your life and your world. Do not sit back and wait for others to create your life. It is solely your responsibility and your boon. No one knows better than you what a life of fulfillment means and looks like to you.

There is no need to wait for the big changes. Start small; just start. We are talking about all areas of your life, be it health, family, love, or abundance. The time for excuses are over, it is the time to make it happen. Do not be fearful about changes in your life. Lead with your intuition and your heart. Coming from a place of love eliminates the fear and indecision. Making the right choices for you will bring you to a place of inner peace and love. This will benefit all who are a part of your life. Lead by example and soon those small changes will become easier and will lead to big changes, which will lead to a more fulfilling life.

You are not meant to struggle. You are meant to thrive. There are changes all around you; do not be that person who regrets standing still. The rewards for taking risks in your life to become a better person and grow will far outweigh the struggles. Change may come easier for some than others; don't let that stop you. In the end, it always works out for the best.

Ride on the winds of change to reach new heights in your life and your world. Remember, change is growing and evolving. It is turning knowledge into wisdom.

AFFIRMATION

I confidently take the steps to make positive changes for my greatest growth.

The Great Goddess

Awaken, my fellow Goddesses!

I am calling you forth to use your voice. For too many centuries, the voice of the Goddess has been silenced. As each of you remember the Goddess within, your voice grows stronger, and in turn, my voice grows stronger.

I am not starting a rebellion. I am calling my sisters to remember. Remember the strength in your voice. Remember the strength in your body, and remember your strength in the community. It is through this community where you are that the Goddess will return. When the Goddess returns, we will have equality, love, and peace on earth. Continue to bring these things into your life and you will continue to bring them to everyone.

AFFIRMATION

I am the living representation of the Goddess.

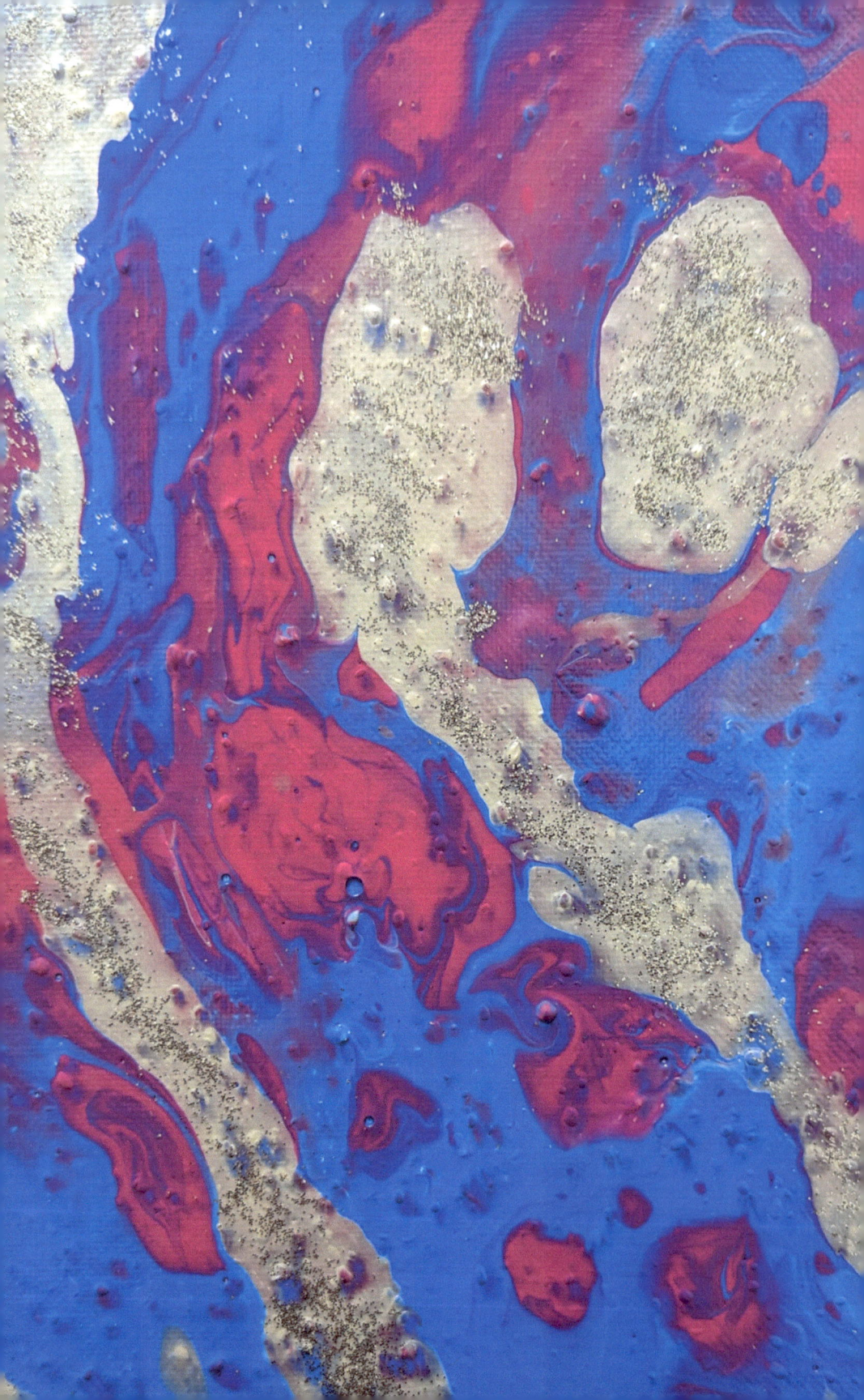

Isis

Release any fears you are still holding on to.

I am the Great Mother. I will not let anything happen to you. You will not be lost in the land. You are here to experience my energy in order to become a clearer channel for my Divine messages that people are thirsting for. You are a precious creation of my womb. I am embodied within you. Your ability to create is unlimited. Fear is the death of creation. Embrace only a life filled with joy and bliss.

The joy and bliss will radiate from every cell of your being. As you radiate this high vibration, you will draw to you high-vibration people. The days of sacrificing yourself for others are gone. It is your time, your life, and your birthright. This is a directive from your Divine Mother.

AFFIRMATION

My ability to create is limitless!

Spirit Guide

Release your anxiety, your fear, and your doubt.

There is no room in your life for these low-vibration energies. You have suffered enough and learned your lessons this lifetime. Now is the time for you to claim your right to a life filled with love and light.

You have touched so many hearts and you have helped so many people without even realizing it. This has brought you to a time and a place in your life that is filled with unlimited possibilities. However, you must release the lower energy forms in order to claim these miracles. These forms can be people, situations, or emotions. Thank them for the lessons you have learned and release them to the light of Creator, for they no longer serve your purpose.

All will be well as you release them in love and light for the highest and best of all. Now is the time for you to claim the life that is waiting for you. For in your service to Spirit, you will have an even greater impact. Raise to the vibration of love and raise the vibration for all.

AFFIRMATION

My life is filled with unlimited possibilities.

The Realm of Guardian Angels

Dear Ones, do not let the mundane tasks of your world get you down.

These areas are all part of a larger plan to teach you balance. Of course, it feels amazing walking around connected to Source and your higher chakras, but you are of this physical world and you must learn to live in balance with the responsibilities of being here. Look at these tasks and responsibilities with gratitude and love. You have been blessed with a place to live, so honor it by keeping it clean. You have been blessed with a physical body to house your beautiful soul, so take pride in providing for it all that it needs to thrive. You have been blessed with the ability to gather with amazing people in your life. Look upon this for the gift that it is, not just another chore to fit into your schedule.

These are just a few of the many blessings in your life. Too many people face them with disdain. We are telling you today that changing your attitude from dreading the mundane to being thankful for all you have received will change your life. You will continue to be blessed with all you need to live in comfort on this earth. The blessings will continue to be showered upon you. Your positive outlook will continue to raise the vibration of your planet. Thus, creating a cycle of blessings and gratitude for all who choose to walk in this path of gratitude and love.

AFFIRMATION

I know how to balance my spiritual world with my physical world.

About the Author

Diane Osvold is a Psychic Medium, Spiritual Advisor, Past Life Regressionist and a Medical Intuitive. She works with individuals to bring them healing and a greater understanding of their connection to spirit. She teaches workshops on Past Lives, Angels and Ascended Masters, Psychic Abilities, and Personal Predictions for a New Year.

Her quest for knowledge of all things spiritual has included workshops and classes all over the world. Diane has studied Angels, Reiki, *Theta Healing™, Kabbalah, and Oracle Card Reading. She has been channeling entities from the spiritual realm since 2017.

Diane discovered her artistic abilities recently through classes by a local artist, and her artwork is featured throughout this book. Diane has a passion for journeying to sacred sites. Her travels have included Bali, Glastonbury, England, and Egypt. Her two favorite sites are Stonehenge and the Sphinx. She is always looking for her next great travel adventure. Diane currently lives in Florida.

To learn more, please visit **www.DianeOsvold.com.**

---

*Theta Healing is a registered trademark by Vianna Stibal

VISIT

www.floweroflifepress.com

www.ingramcontent.com/pod-product-compliance
Lightning Source LLC
Chambersburg PA
CBHW041949240426
43669CB00043B/4